Eat Smart
in
Morocco

Eat Smart
in
MOROCCO

**How to Decipher the Menu
Know the Market Foods
&
Embark on a Tasting Adventure**

Joan Peterson

Illustrated by S. V. Medaris

GINKGO PRESS™ INC

Madison, Wisconsin

Eat Smart in Morocco
Joan B. Peterson

Although the author and publisher have exhaustively researched all sources to ensure the accuracy and completeness of the information contained in this book, we assume no responsibility for errors, inaccuracies, omissions or any inconsistency herein. Any slights of people or organizations are unintentional.

Map lettering is by Gail L. Carlson; cover and insert photographs are by Joan Peterson; author photograph is by Susan Chwae.

The quote by James A. Michener from "This Great Big Wonderful World," from the March 1956 issue of Travel-Holiday Magazine, © 1956 by James A. Michener, is reprinted by permission of the William Morris Agency, Inc. on behalf of the author.

The recipes *Bakoola bil Zitun, Matisha M'sla* and *Khobz Meqli* are from the personal files of Paula Wolfert. ©1999 by Paula Wolfert. Printed by permission of Paula Wolfert.

Publisher's Cataloging in Publication
(Prepared by Quality Books Inc.)
Peterson, Joan (Joan B.)
    Eat smart in Morocco : how to decipher the menu, know
the market foods & embark on a tasting adventure / Joan
Peterson ; illustrated by S. V. Medaris. -- 1st ed.
    p. cm.
    Includes bibliographical references and index.
    Preassigned LCCN: 2001129140
    ISBN 0-9641168-6-3

    1. Cookery, Moroccan. 2. Diet--Morocco. 3. Food
habits--Morocco. 4. Cookery--Morocco. 5. Morocco--
Guidebooks. I. Title.

TX725.M8P48 2001   641.5964
                     QBI01-201017

Printed in the United States of America

To Paula and Souad

Their love and knowledge of Moroccan food
added savor to every page.

Contents

Resources   71

A listing of stores carrying hard-to-find Moroccan foods, travel agencies offering culinary tours, and groups offering opportunities for person-to-person contact through home visits to gain a deeper understanding of the country, including its cuisine.

Helpful Phrases   75

Phrases in English transliterated to Moroccan Arabic, with additional phonetic interpretation, which will assist you in finding, ordering and buying foods or ingredients.

Menu Guide   79

An extensive listing of menu entries in transliterated Moroccan Arabic, with English translations, to make ordering food an easy and immediately rewarding experience.

Foods and Flavors Guide   107

A comprehensive glossary of ingredients, kitchen utensils and cooking methods in transliterated Moroccan Arabic, with English translations.

Preface

> If you reject the food, ignore the customs, fear the
> religion and avoid the people, you might better
> stay home. You are like a pebble thrown into
> water; you become wet on the surface but you are
> never a part of the water.
>
> —JAMES A. MICHENER

As inveterate travelers, my husband David and I have had many adventures around the world. Except for stints as tour directors for the United Service Organization and the International 4-H Youth Exchange, we have traveled independently, relying on our own research and resources. One way we gauge the success of our trips is how familiar we become with the native cuisine. To us, there is no more satisfying way to get immersed in a new culture than to mingle with local people in the places where they enjoy good food and conversation—in their favorite neighborhood cafés, restaurants, picnic spots or outdoor markets. We try to capture the essence of a country through its food, and seek out unfamiliar ingredients and preparations that provide new tastes. By meandering on foot or navigating on local buses, we have discovered serendipitously many memorable eateries away from more heavily trafficked tourist areas. As unexpected but cherished diners, we have had the pleasure of seeing our efforts in learning the cuisine appreciated by the people in ways that make an understanding of each other's language unimportant.

Each trip energizes us as though it were our first; the preparation for a visit becomes about as exciting as the trip itself. Once we determine the destination, we begin to accumulate information—buying relevant guidebooks, raiding the libraries and sifting through our hefty collection of travel articles and clippings for useful data. A high priority for us is the creation of a reference list of the foods, with translations, from our resource materials. For all but a few popular European destinations, however, the amount of information devoted to food is limited. General travel guides and phrase books contain only an overview of the cuisine because they cover so many other subjects of interest to travelers. Not surprisingly, the reference lists we compiled from these sources were inadequate; too many items on menus were unrecognizable. Some menus have translations but these often are more amusing than helpful, and waiters usually cannot provide further assistance in interpreting them. Furthermore, small neighborhood establishments—some of our favorite dining spots—frequently lack menus and post their daily offerings, typically in the native language, on chalkboards outside the door. So unless you are adequately familiar with food words, you may pass up good tasting experiences!

To make dining a more satisfying cultural experience for ourselves and for others, we resolved on an earlier vacation to improve upon the reference lists we always compiled and research the food "on the spot" throughout our next trip. Upon our return, we would generate a comprehensive guidebook, making it easier for future travelers to know the cuisine. The book that resulted from that "next trip" featured the cuisine of Brazil and represented the first in what would be a series of in-depth explorations of the foods of foreign countries; to date we have published five other EAT SMART guides. These cover the cuisines of Turkey, Indonesia, Mexico, Poland and Morocco. Our intention is to enable the traveler to decipher the menu with confidence and shop or browse in supermarkets and fascinating, lively outdoor food and spice markets empowered with greater knowledge.

Our own journeys have been greatly enhanced because we have had new culinary experiences. One of many illustrations of this in Morocco occurred in the fascinating city of Fès, in its ancient medina, or old city, which dates to medieval times. We had engaged the services of a guide as security against losing our way in the medina's labyrinthine passages and missing several important appointments later in the day. After a full morning of exploration in the food and spice *souks* with Amina, we began to think of lunch. I hesitantly inquired about the possibility of finding a small eatery frequented by locals, anticipating that the answer would be similar to the one heard often enough already, "Moroccans dine at home with their families." Amina then added that she wanted us to meet her family and have lunch with them. We happily consented, wondering at the same time if the invitation she extended was impromptu or prearranged with her family during one of her many cell phone conversations earlier in the morning. We'll never know for sure, but judging from what we found at her home—the extended family bustling about, getting ready to preserve meat the traditional way—it probably was planned. Knowing what they were up to, she must have wanted us as food writers to experience some part of the preparation.

Amina's home is a fourth-floor apartment in the Andalusian section of the medina. Above it is a large, screen-enclosed open area, where, we learned later, the meat would be hung out on lines to dry in the sun. To reach the apartment we climbed up a narrow, winding staircase. Several friendly faces welcomed us at the doorway, but our attention initially was riveted on the butchered bull we saw lying on the kitchen floor! This first, brief glance at the animal allowed us to determine that it had already been skinned and that the subcutaneous fat was removed and piled high on a large platter. The head was on the floor near the carcass. Not wanting to appear rude or too non-plussed, we quickly turned our attention to the gracious family members and ignored the evidence of recent carnage.

After having met everyone in the family, we were led into a large room lined with low couches. We sat on a couch with a small table in front of us. Soon, delicious kebabs of the choicest part of the animal—the heart and liver—were served. It's doubtful we've ever enjoyed them any fresher! Young men in the family had cooked the kebabs in the kitchen on long metal skewers over a small charcoal brazier (*kanun*) while we were chatting.

We learned that Amina's family was waiting for the butcher to return and cut the meat so they could process it into *khlii*—spice-cured, sun-dried strips of meat stored in fat until needed. Strips about an inch square and several inches long are rubbed with salt, garlic, and ground cumin and coriander, marinated overnight in this mixture and then dried in the sun. Once dried, the strips are boiled in fat, olive oil and water until the water completely evaporates. They are removed and cooled, put into jars and covered with liquified fat. After the fat solidifies, the jars are tightly closed. Meat preserved this way keeps for over a year and is served in many different dishes.

As our visit was coming to a close, we mentioned to Amina that the carcass must have been a load to lug up all those stairs. She chuckled and made a stepping motion with her hands, indicating the bull had made it up the stairs on his own!

The purpose of the EAT SMART guides is to encourage sampling new and often unusual foods. What better way is there to get to know a culture than through its cuisine? We know informed travelers will be more open to experimentation. The EAT SMART guides also will help steer the traveler away from foods they want to avoid—everyone confesses to disliking something!

This guide has four main chapters. The first provides a history of Moroccan cuisine. It is followed by a chapter with descriptions of regional Moroccan foods. The other main chapters are extensive listings, placed near the end of the book for easy reference. The *Menu Guide* is an alphabetical compilation of menu entries, including more-general Moroccan fare as well as regional specialties. Some not-to-be-missed dishes with country-wide popularity are labeled "national favorite" in the margin next to the menu entry. Some classic regional dishes of Morocco—also not to be missed—are labeled "regional classic." The *Foods & Flavors Guide* contains a translation of food items and terms associated with preparing and serving food. This glossary will be useful in interpreting menus since it is impractical to cover in the *Menu Guide* all the flavors or combinations possible for certain dishes.

Also included in the book is a chapter offering hints on browsing and shopping in the food markets and one with phrases that will be useful in restaurants and food markets to learn more about the foods of Morocco. A chapter is devoted to classic Moroccan recipes. Do take time to experiment with these recipes before departure; it is a wonderful and immediately rewarding way to preview Moroccan food. Most special Moroccan ingredients in these recipes can be obtained in the United States; substitutions for unavailable ingredients are given. Sources for hard-to-find Moroccan ingredients can be found in the *Resources* chapter, which also cites groups that focus on travel to Morocco or offer the opportunity to have person-to-person contact through home visits to gain a deeper understanding of the country, including its cuisine.

At the end of the book is a form that can be used to order additional copies of this book or any of our other EAT SMART guides directly from Ginkgo Press,™ Inc. The back of the form can be used for your comments and suggestions. Ginkgo Press would like to hear from you, our readers, about your culinary experiences in Morocco. Your comments and suggestions will be helpful for future editions of this book.

Safar Said (good traveling) & Bismillah (may you enjoy your meal)!

JOAN PETERSON
Madison, Wisconsin

Acknowledgments

We gratefully acknowledge those who assisted us in preparing this book. Susan M. Peters and Susan Schaefer Davis for help with the transliterations; Kitty Morse and Paula Wolfert for proofreading the *Foods & Flavors Guide* and *Menu Guide;* Meriem Bami, Haja Rabha Bami, Halima Benayad, Abdul Bensaid, Rafih Benjelloun, Rita Benjelloun, Cindy Brown, Susan Schaefer Davis, Brahime Essadrati, Haja Fatema, Mustapha Haddouch, Kamel Hassen, Mohamed Kassi, Fatna Kotni, Zohra El Meterfi, Kitty Morse, Elkifly Najah, Futim-Zohra Oaehdghini, Hicham Ouhirra, Kimberly Ouhirra, Nicole Rio, Jean-Marc Varin and Paula Wolfert for contributing recipes from their private collections; S. V. Medaris for her magical illustrations; Gail Carlson for enlivening our maps with her handwriting; Susan Chwae (Ginkgo Press) for a knockout cover design and a classy photograph of the author; Lanita Haag (Widen Enterprises) for the excellent four-color separations; and Nicol Knappen (Ekeby) for bringing the text neatly to order.

We are indebted to many people for help in identifying regional Moroccan foods and menu items, suggesting itineraries, providing source materials or illustration materials, referring resource people, and proposing ways to make the index more useful. Thanks to Hamid Ahmouch, Paula Bami (Unitours), Jebbar Chahdi, Dustin Cowell, Susan Schaefer Davis, Mustafa Haddouch (Haddouch Gourmet Imports), Jeanette Harries, Ronnie Hess, Tim Mello, Souad Naime, Hicham and Kimberly Ouhirra (Exotica Oils, Inc.), Kitty Morse, Joan Rundo, Nancy Stutzman, Paula Wolfert and Omar Zaher (Travel in Style).

We'd like to thank the following people for introducing us to regional foods, presenting cooking demonstrations or serving as translators in Morocco: Molihsine Abdellatif (translator, Fès), Mbarek Abouelfadel (directeur, L'Institut de Technologie Hôtelière et Touristique, Fès), Mohamed Achalouane (chef de cuisine, Institut de Technologie Hôtelière et Touristique, Marrakech), Driss Ahmouch, Fatima Ahmouch, Hamid Ahmouch (unofficial guide), Hosain Ahmouch, Zahara Ahmouch, Nouassi Amal (student, L'Institut de Technologie Hôtelière et Touristique, Fès), Naima Amouri (chef de cuisine, Palais Salam hotel restaurant, Taroudant), Mehdi Aoullay (professor, Institut de Technologie Hôtelière et Touristique, Marrakech), Meriem Bami, Haj Miloud Bami, Paula Bami (owner, Unitours, Marrakech), Haja Rabha Bami, Abdelkader Berri (manager, Palais Salam hotel and restaurant, Taroudant), Ahmed Derouich (student, L'Institut de Technologie Hôtelière et Touristique, Fès), Chaouqui M. Dkaier (owner/manager Dar Marjana restaurant, Marrakech), Jander Essaadia (student, L'Institut de Technologie Hôtelière et Touristique, Fès), Brahime Essadrati (chef de cuisine, Palais Terrab restaurant, Mèknes), Haja Fatema (chef de cuisine, Palais Mnebhi restaurant), Mohamed Haibi (directeur de etudes, Institut de Technologie Hôtelière et Touristique, Marrakech), Kamel Hassen (sous chef, El Korsan restaurant in the El Minzah hotel, Tangier), Boustila Ibtissam (translator, Ouarzazate), Selwa Mestour Idrissi (secrétaire de direction, El Minzah hotel), Mohamed Kassi (chef de cuisine, La Fibule de Dra^c hotel, Zagora), Ahmed El Khatabi (manager, Palais La Medina restaurant, Fès), Fatna Kotni (chef de cuisine, Dar Marjana restaurant, Marrakech), Amina Lebbar (guide, Fès), Zohra El Meterfi (chef de cuisine, Palais la Medina restaurant, Fès), Najat Mokhtar, Khadija Moutassamem, Elkifly Najah (chef de cuisine/teacher, L'Institut de Technologie Hôtelière et Touristique, Fès), Souad Niame (guide, Marrakech), Rozak Noima (chef, Fint restaurant, Ouarzazate), Futim-Zohra Oaehdoghini (chef de cuisine, Fint restaurant, Ouarzazate), Moulay Ahmed Sentissi (directeur général, Palais Mnebhi restaurant), Haj Abdellatif Terrab (owner, Palais Terrab restaurant, Mèknes), Hamid Trid (directeur général, Fint restaurant, Ouarzazate), Jean-Marc Varin (executive chef, La Tour Hassan Meridian hotel, Rabat), Abdelkrim Zakar (directeur, Institut de Technologie Hôtelière et Touristique, Marrakech) and the Zkhiri family (Yacout restaurant, Marrakech).

Thanks also to the members of the Bstilla Internet Discussion List for useful information on Morocco, Norman and Audrey Stahl, whose unofficial newspaper clipping services kept us well-supplied with timely articles about Morocco, and Dave Nelson for his unflagging encouragement.

And special thanks to Brook Soltvedt, a most perceptive and helpful editor.

Eat Smart
in
Morocco

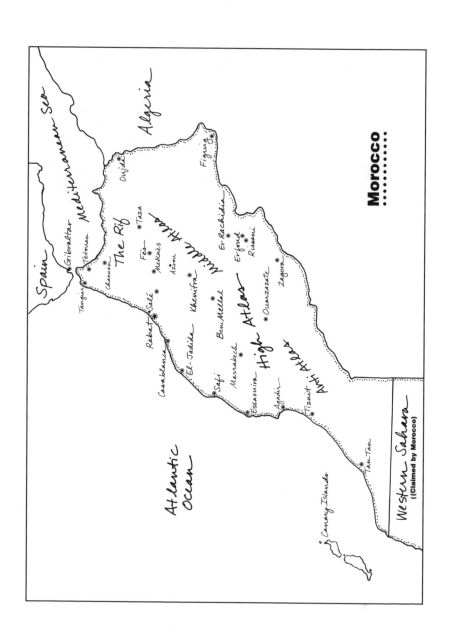

Spain

Mediterranean Sea

Gibraltar

Tangier

Tetouan

Chaouen

The Rif

Oujda

Taza

Fès

Meknès

Azrou

Khenifra

Middle Atlas

Algeria

Figuig

Er-Rachidia

Erfoud

Rissani

Rabat

Salé

Casablanca

El-Jadida

Safi

Beni-Mellal

Marrakech

Ouarzazate

Zagora

Essaouira

High Atlas

Agadir

Tiznit

Anti Atlas

Atlantic Ocean

Tan-Tan

Canary Islands

Western Sahara
((Claimed by Morocco))

Morocco

The Cuisine of Morocco

An Historical Survey

The coastal strip of northern Africa that comprises the modern states of Morocco, Algeria, Tunisia and northwestern Libya is known in Arabic as the Maghreb, which means the place of the sunset, or the west. For several hundred years much of Spain was also part of the Maghreb. Morocco's position at the extreme northwestern end of the region earned it the Arabic name al-Maghreb al-Akhtar, the land farthest west, and it was once the last frontier of Islam.

Morocco's indigenous people, the semi-nomadic Berbers, were known to the Romans as the Mauri. They had little contact with other cultures until about 1200 BC, when seafaring Phoenician traders developed commercial interests along the Mediterranean coastline of North Africa and certain river shores. The defeat of the Phoenicians by the Romans at Carthage in 146 BC brought the land of the Mauri (Mauretania) under Roman rule. During this era, several trade routes running from the Mediterranean coast to sub-Saharan Africa were opened. These routes connected the Berbers in the coastal plains with the peoples of sub-Saharan Africa, and brought another set of cultural influences and foodways to them.

The key event in shaping Morocco's history was the arrival of the Arabs and Islam in the 7th century. In time the Berber clans embraced Islam. Looking to expand Muslim territory in the name of the Prophet, the Arabs and an Islamicized Berber army began in 711 to conquer much of the Iberian peninsula. Moorish Spain became known as al-Andalus (Andalusia). When Spanish-born Muslims and Sephardic Jews were expelled during the Reconquest of Spain by the Christian monarchy in the late 15th century, they returned to Morocco as refugees and brought along their distinctive cultures.

European penetration into Morocco for foreign markets intensified in the 15th century. Portuguese adventurers established themselves in ports along the Mediterranean and Atlantic coasts. The Spanish, English and French also infiltrated the country to advance their causes, and in the process introduced the Western world.

From a culinary point of view, these cross-cultural exchanges occurring over the centuries produced a distinct Moroccan cuisine.

Early History

Several times during the past million years there have been periods of abundant rainfall. The last occurred at the end of the Ice Age, about 12,000 BC, and North Africa enjoyed a wet, tropical climate. By 10,000 BC, people inhabited the region. Large, lush grasslands with abundant game supported a Neolithic hunting society and later a pastoral community of livestock herders in what is now the Sahara Desert. Remarkable insight into this early era of North African history is provided by distinctive prehistoric rock paintings, dating perhaps as early as 6000 BC, which depict negroid hunters with bows and arrows. After about a millenium, people herding cattle, sheep and goats appeared in the drawings.

The early inhabitants harvested wild grain from the grasses of the savannah with sickles and processed it with primitive grinding stones. Indigenous cereals included the wild progenitors of fonio (a type of millet), sorghum and African rice, which grew in shallow, year-round lakes fed by rain. The diet was supplemented with wild fruits, meat and freshwater fish.

The region became inhospitable after about 4000 BC as climate changes gradually led to an arid environment and the desert as we know it today. Habitable areas were confined to scattered oases, which supported specialized agriculture, such as date palm cultivation.

The Berbers

The Berbers have inhabited Morocco longer than any other peoples and are considered its indigenous inhabitants. About 75 percent of present-day Moroccans are of Berber descent. Very little is known about their origin. A heterogeneous, linguistically related population collectively known as Berbers began their movement into North Africa about 2000 BC. They moved in waves into the coastal tract that extended across the continent from Egypt to the Atlantic Ocean between the Sahara Desert and the Mediterranean. Evidence suggests that they began their westward migration into North Africa from Southwestern Asia. Others migrated to the desert and joined the oasis dwellers, who, it is thought, were descendants of the aboriginal black population of the savannah. Scholars speculate that interbreeding between the ancient aboriginal people and the Berbers gave rise to the Harratin, the black-skinned inhabitants who live in pre-Saharan and Saharan oases south of Morocco's Atlas Mountains.

Our understanding of the Berbers from ancient times is derived from writings of the people who occupied their land. This indigenous civilization was already well established when maritime Phoenicians from the coastal cities of Tyre and Sidon in present-day Lebanon began to establish an extensive network of trading stations for ore and salt along the Mediterranean and Atlantic coasts of North Africa about 1200 BC. Lixus, Tangier, Essaouira, and Tetouan are some of the present-day Moroccan cities that began as ancient trading posts.

Initially, the influence of the Phoenician traders on the Berbers was limited to the tribes living in coastal villages and along waterways in the interior. Inland tribes were relatively unaffected, and continued their ancestral way of life, tending herds and cultivating crops on simple farms. Permanent Phoenician settlements, however, were to exert a more profound cultural influence beyond their immediate vicinity. Carthage, founded by the Phoenicians on the coast of present-day Tunisia in 814 BC, later became a powerful independent state. At one point it controlled the North African coastline, parts of Spain and the islands of Sicily, Corsica and Sardinia.

Because of the Phoenician presence, the Berbers were exposed to advanced farming and horticultural techniques, and were introduced to many new crops, including the pomegranate, olive, grape, date and fig. They labored in vineyards and orchards, and pressed olives to obtain their much-prized oil for use in cooking and medicine. Inhabitants of coastal cities probably were engaged in the Phoenician business of preserving fish with salt to make a spicy, fermented liquid called *garum* from the flesh and entrails of fish, primarily tuna. This concoction, favored by the Romans, was exported in special amphorae.

The Berbers came under Roman influence after the fall of Carthage in 146 BC. The rapidly expanding Roman Empire, aspiring to supremacy of the Mediterranean Sea, overthrew the Carthaginians after three bloody struggles—the Punic wars—were fought. The Romans took over Mauretania and

Numidia, the two prominent Berber kingdoms in North Africa at the time. The conquerors were preoccupied with protecting their interests along the coastal trade routes and spent little energy on the hinterlands until 42 AD, when they took direct administrative control. Mauretania was divided into two provinces: Mauretania Tingitana to the west, which coincided with much of present-day Morocco, and Mauretania Caesariensis to the east, which is now (primarily) the northern part of present-day Algeria.

The agrarian economy of the North African provinces greatly expanded as the occupied lands were intensively cultivated to feed the Roman Empire. North Africa supplied about 70 percent of Rome's wheat, and acquired the title "the granary of Rome." Olive trees were planted on marginal, fallow lands useless for growing wheat. Ancient stone olive presses, along with drains and vats for separation and storage, can be seen today in the ruins of Volubilis, the notable capital of Mauretania Tingitana near Meknès. In Lixus, stone remnants of the once-flourishing Roman factories that made *garum,* including carved mixing tubs, are testimony to the popularity of this nutritious culinary seasoning and elixir made in earlier times by the Phoenicians in North Africa to satisfy Roman palates. This salty, fishy liquid embellished most foods, including fruit.

Under the Romans, the Berbers of the coastal plains became urbanized. Some worked as tenant farmers on Roman estates. Those living in the interior resisted assimilation, continuing their own way of life in the mountains and deserts. Powerful native chieftains remained in charge of local affairs, appeasing the Romans by providing tribute and soldiers.

The hardy riding camel was introduced in Mauretania toward the end of the Roman occupation. It became the common pack animal and revolutionized transportation, enabling Berber tribes to more easily cross the vast Sahara Desert on the trade routes connecting the Mediterranean coast and sub-Saharan Africa. Traders controlled the movement of salt from dry lake basins in the desert to tropical Africa. In exchange for this vital commodity, West African gold and spices such as pepper were transported to the Mediterranean coast.

Early in the 5th century AD, Roman authority in North Africa weakened. An army of Germanic Vandals, sweeping down from Spain, seized power in 429 AD. They were more interested in piracy than overseeing the hinterlands, however, and had no lasting impact. The area reverted to its indigenous Berber rulers. In 533 AD, the Byzantines briefly established a North African empire. More than a century would elapse before the most significant change in the Berber way of life would be wrought by the next wave of invaders—the Arabs.

Festivals and pilgrimages have always been an important part of Berber life. Some Berber contributions to Morocco's culinary heritage are rooted in the tribal assembly, called *ammougar* or *moussem*. Traditionally it has an agricultural basis and is held near the sanctuary of a local holy man or saint (*marabout*) of the tribe. The classic Berber specialty of spit-roasted whole lamb (*mechoui*) is served as part of the feast, or *diffa*, following the celebration. The meat typically cooks over a smoldering fire for several hours. Frequent bastings with butter seasoned with garlic, cumin and paprika produce a crispy crust with succulent, moist meat inside. Morsels are pulled from the roast with the fingers and dipped in ground cumin and coarse salt.

The Berbers are credited with developing a method of preserving strips of spice-cured meat, which provided a stockpile of food for them that kept for over a year. Meat (primarily beef) is preserved in the same manner today. It is cured overnight in a rub of salt, garlic, ground cumin and coriander, and dried on lines in the sun for several days. The sun-dried strips are then boiled

Old postcard (circa 1900) showing Moroccan women making couscous (*seksu*) granules. A mixture of coarse and fine particles of semolina are moistened with water and rubbed with a circular motion of the fingers against the bottom of a round, flat dish (*gsaa*).

in water and animal fat until all the water has evaporated. The preserved strips (*khlii*) are stored in solidified fat until needed. Several everyday preparations containing *khlii* include certain stews, such as *ᶜdes bil gerᶜa hamra wa khlii,* which features lentils, pumpkin and spice-cured, sun-dried strips of beef. *Khlii* is also a favorite filling in flat breakfast pastries (*rghaif*).

Other notable Berber dishes include *byesar,* a hearty, thick purée of broad (fava) beans topped with drizzled olive oil, paprika and cumin. Similar dishes based on grains, legumes and vegetables are still the mainstay of the diet, often reflecting a subsistence economy and harsh living conditions. Examples are *azenbu,* a seasoned porridge made of a non-wheat grain, particularly barley, and *baddaz,* a porridge made with cornmeal to which boiled, chopped greens may be added. Yeast-raised semolina pancakes (*beghrir*) cooked on one side only in an unoiled earthenware dish are also a Berber specialty. The "uncooked" side characteristically is riddled with tiny holes. *Therfist* is unleavened Berber flatbread made in sheets. The Berber habit of using steam to cook certain foods has left its mark on Moroccan cookery. An example is the popular dish of cooked greens (*bakoola*), which traditionally is made by steaming the nutritious, wild, spinach-like plant called mallow.

Some scholars conclude that Morocco's national dish, couscous (*seksu*), was developed by the Berbers. This is based on the discovery of ancient couscous vessels in tombs dating to the reign of Masinissa, a Berber king of Numidia in the 2nd century BC. Both savory and sweet preparations of couscous are made. All have as their basis pasta granules—also called couscous (*seksu*)—formed from wheat and other grains, which are steamed, mounded into a cone and topped with meat, vegetables, or cinnamon and sugar.

The round, two-piece earthenware cooking utensil (*tagine*) that traditionally is used to cook and serve Moroccan stews is of Berber origin. It has a shallow base and a tall, conical lid pierced with a small hole to allow steam to escape. A stew made in this cooking utensil also is called a *tagine.*

The Arabs

The city of Mecca in western Saudi Arabia was a major commercial and religious center on several ancient spice routes. Located between the Persian and Byzantine Empires, it was a place of pilgrimage long before the birth of the Prophet Mohammad there in 570 AD. Arab pilgrims gathered annually in Mecca for a month-long fair in order to conduct trade and worship sacred images of hundreds of deities housed in a holy sanctuary in the center of the city.

As a young man, the Prophet Mohammed earned his living in the camel caravan trade, eventually marrying his employer, a wealthy spice merchant. He became preoccupied with religious questions and frequently withdrew to a desert retreat to meditate on the meaning of life and the pagan practices of his kinsmen in Mecca. By his own accounts, in his 40th year he received revelations from the angel Gabriel to restore the worship of the One True God, Allah. He was convinced that he had been ordained a Prophet and given the mission of converting his countrymen from their pagan tribal beliefs and moral decadence. The religion he founded—Islam—united the devout and the state under the will of God. Followers of Islam, the Muslims, submitted to the word of Allah and began to spread the faith to the rest of the world through the *jihad,* or "holy war."

The Muslim Empire expanded rapidly as the Arab armies brought Islam westward from Mecca. Within 10 years western Asia was subdued. North

Tagine, a two-piece, glazed earthenware cooking dish consisting of a flat, shallow-rimmed round bottom and a conical cover. It is used to cook and serve Moroccan stews of the same name.

7

Africa was brought into the fold after 50 years and considerable Berber resistance. By 710 AD, Berber tribes in coastal towns of Morocco began converting to the new faith. Many Berbers, however, resisted Arab domination, and retreated into the Atlas Mountains or into the Sahara Desert. Aligned with Arabs only by Islam, Berbers proudly retained their cultural identity, and kept certain pre-Islamic religious activities, such as the worship of *marabouts* and the veneration of their tombs, especially in the countryside and mountains.

For centuries, Arab merchants had a monopoly on the spice trade. They invented clever and exaggerated tales about dangers that they had experienced in mysterious far-away places when obtaining spices, in order to prevent others from finding their sources. The spice trade also facilitated the rapid spread of Islam. After the Muslim conquest, Arab traders traveled the entire length of a trade route, no longer teaming up with intermediaries who would carry spices and other goods over part of the route. Spices transported to Morocco included cinnamon, cassia, black pepper and long pepper, a pungent berry resembling an elongated peppercorn. Morocco's famous exotic spice blend, called *ras l-hanut* in Arabic, is a legacy of the Arab spice traders. The name means "head of the shop" and the mixture is a spice shop's personal (and usually secret) blend of a myriad of ground spices and herbs.

As Arabs explored farther afield, the culinary variety they brought to Moroccan food likewise increased. The pre-Islamic diet of the nomadic Arabs consisted primarily of dates, barley, sheep's or camel's milk and, occassionally, meat. This austere fare was enriched as the power of Islam spread, and new foods and dishes from conquered lands were introduced to the Arabs and subsequently added to the subsistence diet of the Berbers of Morocco.

The Arabs overran the Persian Empire in the middle of the 7th century AD and incorporated it into the caliphate—the government of the Prophet's successor, who was the supreme earthly leader of Islam. A rich Arabic literature records the everyday foods and gastronomic excesses of the Arab aristocrats in the courts at Damascas and Baghdad. We learn that the culinary technique of thickening sweet and savory sauces with powdered nuts, such as walnuts, almonds and pistachios, came from Persia. The Arabs also brought from Persia the custom of mixing the flavors of meat with spices, fruit and nuts, and using this as a filling for pastries made with thin sheets of dough. A crown jewel in the Moroccan menu is *bestila,* a large and elaborate, saffron-flavored pie served as the first course in a celebration feast. It contains many ultrathin, round sheets of pastry dough called *warka,* which the Arabs learned to make in Persia. Pastry sheets are layered with pieces of cooked squab (often with bones), a lemony egg sauce and toasted almonds. After the pie is baked, its surface is sprinkled with powdered sugar and decorated with stripes or lattices drawn with cinnamon. Some culinary historians, however, feel it more likely that *bestila* exemplifies the rich cuisine of Moorish Spain, and that its name comes from the Spanish word *pastilla,* meaning pastry. History records that *trid,* a more primitive version of *bestila,* was the Prophet Mohammad's favorite dish. *Trid* is made with thin, circular sheets of somewhat oily pastry dough that are stacked with some sauce between them. Stewed meat is placed on top of the stack.

The custom of coloring foods yellow is attributed to the Arabs. Wealthy Moroccans use saffron to obtain this color and enjoy at the same time the exquisite flavor it imparts to their dishes. Those of more modest means use a powdered colorant consisting primarily of turmeric with just a hint of saffron. This colorant is available commercially in small paper packets, and, when stirred into stews and other dishes, turns the food yellow.

Arabs also influenced the manner of eating in Morocco. Food is brought to the mouth with the tips of three fingers of the right hand: the thumb and the first and second index fingers. A piece of bread is used as a utensil to help take food from a communal dish placed in the center of the table.

The pattern of daily life changed significantly for Islamicized Berbers. They now lived by the lunar calendar and participated in several important annual Muslim celebrations. Ramadan is a 30-day holy period commemorating the time during which God was said to reveal the Koran to Mohammad. For 30 days the faithful fast between sunrise and sunset in repentence for their sins of the past year. Their fast is broken at the end of each day by eating a thick soup (attributed to the Berbers) called *harira,* which is made of lentils and chickpeas with lamb or meatballs. *Harira* typically is eaten with a special spoon (*mgerfa*) carved from lemon or orange wood. Usual soup accompaniments are dates or sweet pastries resembling irregular coils of ribbons (*shebbakiya*).

Another Muslim holy day is ᶜId le-Kbir, the Festival of Sacrifice. It commemorates the near sacrifice of Isaac by his father, Abraham. God spared the child, allowing a lamb to be sacrificed instead. Throughout the country, those who can afford it slaughter a sheep. Several lamb dishes traditionally appear on tables during this four-day festival. Among them are various lamb stews (*tagines*), including *douara,* a stew of lamb giblets (heart, liver and tripe) in a sauce of tomatoes, onions and garlic; *boulfaf,* grilled kebabs of lamb liver wrapped in caul; and *hergma,* a stew of lamb's trotters with coarsely ground wheat and chickpeas.

The Moors

Tingis (present-day Tangier) was occupied by the Arabs in 709 AD. It became the base from which the conquest of the Iberian peninsula was begun in 711 by an army of Islamicized Berbers led by the military leader Tarik ibn Ziyad, one of the first Berbers to convert to Islam. Gibraltar is named after him, a corruption of the Arabic name Jebel Tarik meaning Tarik's Mountain. An Arab army helped complete the conquest of the barbaric Visigoths in Spain. Within four years almost all of Spain was occupied by Muslims, who were regarded as liberators by the Jews and Christians living in the occupied lands.

Muslim Arabs and Berbers crossed the Straits of Gibraltar and settled in the conquered empire—called Al-Andalus (Andalusia), or "land of the

Mgerfa, a wooden spoon or ladle, typically carved from a piece of orange or lemon wood. The classic soup served at the end of each day to break the fast during Ramadan—*harira*—is eaten with a *mgerfa*. It has a characteristic round, deep bowl and a straight cylindrical handle with a tapered end.

Vandals," in Arabic. Their culture became known as Moorish. They created a civilization of extraordinary intellectual and artistic brilliance. The cities of Córdoba, Toledo, Seville and Granada attracted scholars from all parts of Europe.

The Moors notably improved the existing agricultural system by building extensive irrigation channels to increase the productivity of the land. They were familiar with waterwheels, aqueducts, fertilizers, and grafting. To the major crops already growing in Andalusia—wheat and olives—they added fruits such as oranges, lemons, mulberries, peaches, apricots, figs, grapes and pomegranates. Also introduced to the menu were eggplants, artichokes, almonds, sugar cane, rice and many spices, including saffron, cinnamon, cumin and black pepper. The Moors also established the Persian practice of combining meats with fruit, nuts with fruit, and the blending of sweet and savory tastes.

Moors populated Spain for nearly seven centuries, but never established a stable central government. Successive Arab and Berber dynasties ruled Morocco, and some extended their power over Moorish Spain, bringing both within a single empire. As dynasties disintegrated, Christian rulers in non-Muslim northern Spain began to recapture the south. Toledo fell in 1085 and Córdoba in 1236. The last Muslim stronghold in Andalúsia—Granada— was lost to the Catholic monarchs Ferdinand and Isabella in 1492.

Moors unwilling to abandon their religion and convert to Christianity were driven from Spain. Many emigrated to Morocco, and the foodways they brought with them were an important influence on Moroccan cuisine. Dishes of Moorish Spain were a fusion of Berber and Arab elements that were enhanced during the lengthy period of Moorish rule in Andalusia. The culinary legacy from southern Spain included the classic one-dish meal called *paella.* Today this dish of saffron-flavored rice with an assortment of seafoods and meats is quintessentially Spanish, but its gastronomic roots are Moorish. *Paella,* as well as *tapas* (Spanish canapés), can be found on menus in the regions of northern Morocco where the Spanish influence is still strong. Baked goods made with almonds, eggs and sugar, and honeyed sweets recall a Persian heritage and Andalusian fondness for almonds. The cold soup based on garden vegetables, *gazpacho* (meaning "soaked bread" in Arabic), started out as a soupy Moorish mixture of garlic, olive oil, lemon juice and bread. Spanish *gazpacho* containing tomatoes and green peppers evolved when these new vegetables were brought to Spain as part of the Columbian exchange following the post-Reconquest discovery of the

Americas. Moroccans often use the New World vegetables in salads, which, for them, are raw or cooked preparations that have been sweetened or flavored with spices.

The Jews

Jews have been in Morocco since antiquity. History records a sizeable population of Jews in the Roman state of Mauretania. Some are said to have come with the Phoenicians; others arrived earlier, after the fall of the Temple of Jerusalem in 70 AD. Still others were Berbers who converted during Roman times. As with the Moors, Sephardic Jews in Spain who refused to convert to Christianity were forced to flee after the Reconquest. Many of them were descendants of the Jews who had left Morocco to live in Andalusia centuries earlier. Jewish "exiles" relocating to Morocco went to urban centers, such as present-day Tangier and Tetouan on the northern coast, and Fès. By the time this influx of Jews from Spain took place, Moroccan Jews residing in major urban centers of Morocco had been required to relocate to special enclosed quarters (ghettos). This ostensibly was to protect them from the increasing hostility of the population, since Jews were reported to be the only remaining non-Muslim group. A settlement area was called *melha,* the Arabic name for salt. This name supposedly derives from one of the occupations imposed on these Jews—the preservation by salting of severed heads that were taken as war booty for display outside the city gates.

Jewish cuisine throughout the world is based on dietary laws (kashruth) concerning how foods are prepared. Based on these laws, Jews adapted their eating habits to the foods of their adopted lands and substituted ingredients from available products when necessary. The Jews of Spain brought to Morocco their tradition of preparing a slow-cooked, one-dish meal containing beans or chickpeas, potatoes and meat, which was served for lunch on the Sabbath (Saturday). It is cooked in a tightly sealed baking dish on Friday and kept warm over ashes until the next day, honoring the religious rule that no work be done on the day of rest. In Morocco the dish became known as *dafina,* meaning "covered" in Arabic, and lamb is often substituted for beef. The dish also includes eggs cooked in the shell (called *huevos haminados* in Spanish), and rice or bread dumplings that bake in a foil or cheesecloth bag placed in the middle of the pot. No one was to open the baking dish before the *dafina* was served.

The Sephardic Jews brought with them their fondness for vegetables, oranges and sugar, and their habit of cooking with olive oil. Their remarkable ways with food continue to be applauded. Jewish-style pickles and marinated vegetables are highly esteemed. Olive oil is often added to the pickling brine, and the pickled product—small cucumbers and tiny eggplants, for example— is extraordinary. Moroccan Sephardic cookery includes the use of white truffles, especially prized mushrooms, in dishes such as lamb stews. The Sephardic Jews also are recognized for their ability to distill fine liqueurs from fruits. Some of these products, such as *mahya,* a colorless aniseed-flavored fig brandy, are available commercially.

The Europeans

Spanish (Castilian) expeditions began raiding Moroccan ports as Muslim power declined in Spain. Motivated by revenge against Muslim rule and clamoring for retaliation against piracy, the Spaniards seized several northern coastal cities, including Tetouan in 1399, and frequently attacked other towns on the Atlantic. After the fall of Granada, marking the end of Muslim

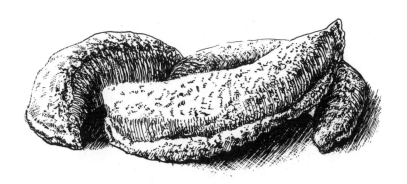

These crescent-shaped *ka'b el ghzal* or "gazelle's horns" are one of several pastries filled with much-loved almond paste. Only a very thin shell of pastry encases the filling. Orange-flower water is added to the dough and often to the almond paste as well. A variety of this pastry that is dipped in orange-flower water and coated with powdered sugar is called *ka'b el ghzal m'fenned.*

domination in Spain, the enclave of Mellila was taken. The Portuguese captured Ceuta in 1415, which passed to Spain in 1580, and by the end of the 15th century established fortresses along most of the Atlantic coast of Morocco. The strategic city of Tangier on the Straits of Gibraltar was seized in 1471. Portuguese influence waned within a century as her interests elsewhere overseas greatly increased.

In the 19th and early 20th centuries, European colonial expansion accelerated. Morocco was among a handful of places on the African continent still relatively unexploited, and the economic potential tempted European powers. Morocco used the intense rivalry among Britain, Spain, France and Germany to her advantage, pitting the countries against each other. Following years of political intrigue, two powers emerged—France and Spain. The major winner was France. A large central zone representing most of the country was governed as a French protectorate beginning in 1912. Tangier was declared an international zone. Spain's sphere of influence comprised part of the Western Sahara annexed in 1884, and small enclaves on the northern coast, which became Spanish protectorates. Moroccan nationalist sentiment began to appear in the 1930s, and in 1956 Morocco regained its independence. The status of the Western Sahara, however, is still in limbo. Morocco laid claim to the area when Spain sought its autonomy,

Fresh spearmint (*Mentha viridis*). Moroccans typically add sprigs of mint and chunks of sugar cut from a large loaf to steeping tea. Spearmint is the commonest variety used and vendors sell it most everywhere.

and a referendum on Moroccan rule versus self-government has been delayed by disputes over voter eligibility.

One of the most important European contributions to the Moroccan larder occurred in the early part of the sixteenth century as a result of the Columbian Exchange—the diffusion of plants and animals between the New and Old Worlds as a result of Old World exploration in the Americas. In the vegetable category alone, new additions included corn, tomatoes, potatoes, sweet potatoes, beans, sweet bell peppers, chile peppers, pumpkin and squash. Portuguese explorers brought spices such as nutmeg, mace, cloves and cinnamon from Southeast Asia to Europe and then to Morocco. The French influence is especially strong in the cities, where croissants or other pastries are sold in pâtissiere shops and enjoyed with espresso. A French connection is also seen in the use of mushrooms in many dishes. The country's beloved national drink is a British contribution. British merchants introduced Chinese green tea in the 1800s. The Moroccan touch was to steep it with fresh sprigs of spearmint and pieces of sugar cut from a large loaf.

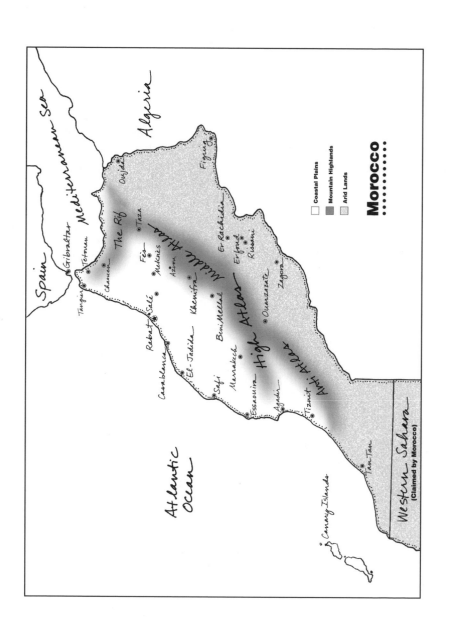

Regional Moroccan Food

A Quick Tour of Moroccan Foods and Their Regional Variations

Moroccan Food in a Nutshell

Morocco's adventurous cuisine is based on the liberal use of spices. Yet it should not be thought of as spicy, because the rich, aromatic seasonings are subtly married to the healthy foods they enhance. Typical spices include cumin, paprika, cinnamon, saffron, turmeric and dried ginger. Other important seasonings are parsley, cilantro, onions, garlic and cayenne pepper. The complex mixture called *ras l-hanut,* which is a proprietary concoction made by spice shop owners, is also widely used in cooking. It contains herbs, common spices, such as those mentioned above, and many exotic additions, including components thought to be aphrodisiacs (see p. 125).

Several ingredients are essential to Moroccan cooking. Lemons preserved in salt and lemon juice impart a unique, pungent flavor to salads and stews of fish or meat, especially chicken (see recipes, pp. 56–57). All sorts of olives pickled in aromatics are nibbled as snacks, added to salads or cooked in stews, frequently in combination with preserved lemons. Moroccans appreciate olive oil and use a generous amount of it in their dishes, mopping up the excess with bread. Aged, salted butter (*smen*), often mixed with dried herbs, provides a strong, cheesy flavor (an acquired taste) to couscous and certain sauces and soups. *Smen* that is many years old is a coveted commodity that is saved for special occasions. A thick, fiery paste of Tunisian origin (*harissa*) is served as a relish on the side. It is made with dried, hot red chile peppers, olive oil and garlic, and is added to dishes according to taste. Flavored waters distilled from fresh rose and orange blossoms are used in a variety of sweet and savory dishes. Rose water (*ma ward*) is added to certain pastries, and orange-flower water (*ma zher*) is put in some pastries, cakes, beverages, puddings and salads. Both fragrant waters also are used as a refreshing perfume to rub on the hands after a meal.

Perhaps the central ingredient of Moroccan cuisine is *seksu* (couscous), the Berber word that refers to both the dry grain product—small granules made of semolina—as well as a preparation of granules steamed and often covered with a *tagine,* or stew, with the whole arranged into a pyramid. Couscous is Morocco's national dish, and as such there are countless variations of it, including sweet ones served for dessert. Traditionally it is served on Friday, the Islamic Sabbath, as a one-course family meal following the early afternoon prayers. For a *diffa,* or celebration feast, it is the last of many courses preceding dessert. *Seksu* Beidaoui is the classic Casablanca-style dish of couscous with seven vegetables and sometimes meat (see recipe, p. 51, and photo, color insert). The vegetables are arranged in radial fashion on a mound of couscous. If meat is included, it will be placed on the peak of the mound. It is considered good luck to have seven vegetables in the preparation, but more or less than that also will be encountered. The name of the dish reflects the city's name in Arabic, Dar-el-Beida (white house). A favorite sweet couscous dish is *seffa*. The couscous is patted into a cone-shaped mound and then decorated with nuts and dried fruit. Radial lines of cinnamon are drawn from the top to the bottom of the cone, and powdered sugar crowns the peak. Small bowls of milk or buttermilk typically accompany *seffa*.

Couscous most frequently is made of semolina from durum wheat, but preparations also are made of other grains, including barley, corn and millet. Families traditionally serve couscous in a large communal dish. It is eaten with the fingers, which looks easy, but isn't. A small amount of couscous with bits of the other ingredients is picked up with the thumb and first two fingers of the right hand, and transferred to the palm of the hand. With gentle movement of the cupped hand, the food is tossed up and down, which quickly produces a neat little ball (if one is experienced) that is popped into the mouth with the same fingers used to take it from the bowl.

Moroccans have elevated basic stew cookery to an art form. Both meaty and meatless stews of seemingly infinite variety are cooked to perfection with the help of a dual-purpose, two-piece, glazed earthenware cooking dish. It consists of a flat, shallow-rimmed round bottom and a distinctive conical cover. The earthenware utensil and the aromatic stew cooked within it share the same name—*tagine*. The cover, perforated with a tiny hole for excess steam to escape, is designed to direct rising vapors back down into the stew to keep it moist and to intensify its flavor as it gently simmers over low heat. When the food is cooked, this sleek, practical cookware turns into a lidded serving platter. It is placed in the middle of a small, low dining table where it is within reach of all diners, who eat communally from the same central dish.

In a traditional Moroccan kitchen, the stove most often used to cook a *tagine* is an individual-size, unglazed, round ceramic charcoal brazier (*kanun*) placed on the floor. Its upper rim has three short projections that help keep the *tagine* in place. Commercial heating units using propane gas also operate at floor level. Fortunately, the ceramic cookware can be used at low settings on a Western gas stovetop and in an oven. The nicely decorated *tagine* illustrated on p. 7 was purchased in Safi. Many stews have been cooked in it on the stovetop, including those that were taste tested for this guidebook. See *Tastes of Morocco,* p. 41, for recipes.

Four basic sauces are characteristic of stew (*tagine*) cookery. Each has a handful of requisite ingredients to which cooks frequently add other flavorings to personalize it. Sauces are not cooked separately. They are created as a stew simmers, through the melding of cooking juices and added spices and seasonings, and develop character through reduction. The four classics are *m'hammer,* a red sauce containing paprika, cumin and butter; *m'qualli,* a yellow sauce with saffron, ginger and olive oil and/or peanut oil; *k'dra,* a yellow sauce made with meat stock, aged butter (*smen*), onions, pepper, butter and saffron; and *m'chermel,* a red sauce made by combining these three sauces in various proportions.

Honey-sweetened mixtures enliven several meat dishes. *Tafaya* is a personal favorite. It includes lots of sliced red onions sautéed until limp and then cooked with honey, raisins, almonds, cinnamon, saffron and sometimes a little rose water. The caramelized mixture is used as a topping on several meat dishes, such as the tasty one with lamb called *tagine lham tafaya.* Hard-boiled egg wedges garnish similar Andalusian-style dishes of lamb of the same name (see *tagine lham tafaya,* color insert). *Matisha m^csla* is a tomato purée or jam, sweetened with honey, which is used as a sauce with meat or as a preserve (see recipe, p. 45).

Moroccans love meat and consume it as often as their budget allows. Meat is *halal,* or ritually slaughtered. Poultry is eaten most often, with chicken the most common bird on the menu. Multi-colored chickens are much preferred because their meat is more flavorful than that of the all-white breed that is penned and fed feed. Other relished birds include squab (young pigeon), turkey and cornish hen. Meat is stewed, roasted, braised and browned, and steamed.

Morocco's sumptuous and justly famous culinary masterpiece is *bestila,* an exquisite, multilayered squab pie served as the first course of a *diffa,* or celebration feast. It is made with many ultrathin, round sheets of pastry dough called *warka* (see *bestila,* p. 110). The filling has pieces of cooked squab (often with bones), a lemony egg sauce and sweetened, toasted almonds to nicely complement the flavor of the meat. Chicken can be substituted for the more traditional squab. An outstanding chicken stew that quickly becomes a favorite of foreigners is *djaj m'qualli bil hamd marked wa zitun,* chicken with preserved lemons and olives and in a sauce flavored with ginger and saffron (see recipes, pp. 56–57). Another first-rate preparation using chicken is *trid,* which is a dish made with thin, circular sheets of baked pastry dough layered in a *tagine* with sauce between layers and stewed chicken on top of the stack (see photo, color insert). When chicken and squab are stuffed, the traditional stuffings include rice- or couscous-based mixtures with raisins and chopped almonds. Sweet poultry dishes include *djaj bil tmer,* honeyed chicken with dates (see recipe, p. 58) and *djaj bil ᶜassal wa romman wa luz,* cornish hen with honey, pomegranate juice and toasted almonds (see recipe, p. 59).

One of many live snails (*bebbush*) crawling around in enormous baskets in the medina in Fès, destined for the soup pot. The popular dish of steamed snails in broth has been sold by the same street vendor for over forty years in the *souk.*

Lamb is number one among the red meats. It is stewed, spit-roasted, grilled and steamed. *Mechoui,* lamb roasted the Berber way, is renowned. A whole lamb is spit-roasted over hot embers for several hours and basted frequently with butter seasoned with garlic, cumin and paprika. When done properly, the meat is moist and tender, and the skin dark and crispy. Morsels are picked from the roasted lamb with the fingers and dipped in ground cumin and coarse salt. It traditionally is served as part of a banquet that follows a tribal celebration (*moussem*).

The popularity of the *kabab* (meat grilled on skewers) is reflected in the number of grills present in outdoor markets and in the town eateries. These grills tend to be rectangular and made of metal. *Quodban* is a kebab with small chunks of lamb, often interspersed with pieces of fat. Skewered giblets, mainly liver, also are favored. Moroccan kebabs ordinarily do not have vegetables such as tomatoes, peppers, onions or mushrooms threaded on the skewer between the meat or giblets, but international versions do and they will be offered on menus as well (see recipe, p. 55; it can be made the Moroccan way by omitting the vegetables). *Boulfaf* is a kebab with pieces of fresh lamb's liver seasoned with cumin, paprika and cayenne pepper and individually wrapped in sheep's caul. A kebab with well-seasoned ground meat (*kefta*) wrapped around a skewer like a sausage is another choice. The meat most often is lamb, but it can be a mixture of lamb and beef, or even beef alone (see photo, color insert).

A basic entry in the stew category is *tagine kabab maghdour,* a dish of meatballs in a tomato-based sauce with onions and garlic, and seasoned with paprika, cumin and cayenne pepper. *Tagine kabab maghdour bil bid* is the same dish with the addition of eggs that are poached right in the sauce in the cooking dish just before serving (see recipe, p. 48). A similar stew, with or without eggs, is made with chunks of lamb rather than meatballs. Again, beef will be used in some restaurants in place of the more popular lamb. The words *maghdour kabab* in the name of these dishes means "cheating" kebabs, acknowledgment of the fact that the meat has not been grilled on skewers. *Lham bil berquq wa luz* is a flavorful lamb stew with a sweet topping of prunes, toasted almonds and sesame seeds. It is just one of many meat dishes with a sweet touch provided by a honeyed fruit or vegetable. An unusual dish to look for is the intriguing *sharᶜriya medfoun,* which is a nest of steamed vermicelli with stewed meat hidden within it (see recipe, p. 47).

Beef is most visible in the form of *khlii,* spice-cured, sun-dried strips of meat stored in fat. The preserved meat is cooked in everyday stews with vegetables, with eggs or couscous, and as a filling in flat, savory breakfast pastries collectively known as *rghaif.* Goat, rabbit, camel and game such as partridge may be available in some markets.

A visit to the butchers' quarter in a *souk* in Morocco, and those in many other countries in the world for that matter, can be a daunting experience for those accustomed to buying their meat in neat plastic-wrapped packages. Freshly skinned carcasses hang from hooks in the stalls or sprawl over counter tops, with miscellaneous heaps of heads, hooves and assorted viscera nearby. Large, eye-catching sheets of caul (omentum), the lacy, fatty membrane that surrounds the stomach and other internal organs, are draped over poles. Moroccans avoid eating meat from female animals, believing it both unhealthy and unsavory. Some declare they can taste the difference between meat from male and female animals, even those of comparable age, and boast that they could easily pass a blind taste test to prove it. This explains why butchered animals in markets typically are males, still bearing testicles as proof that the meat is not from females. If anyone wants to purchase just the testicles, the butcher will not sell them because the (sexual) origin of the remaining meat will no longer be certain.

Morocco is especially well supplied with fish and seafood, a much-appreciated bonus attributable to its lengthy coastline. The catch of the day might include red mullet, gray mullet, several types of sea bream, monkfish, sea bass, sardines, anchovies, tuna, swordfish, squid, shrimp, mussels and oysters. Freshwater fish also are important. Unfortunately, the popular shad is becoming a rarity today because its habitat (river estuaries) has been jeopardized (see p. 33).

Almost all fish preparations include the classic, highly seasoned "dry" marinade called *chermula,* which varies from region to region and is likely to contain finely chopped onion, garlic, cilantro, flat-leaf parsley, saffron, paprika, hot red pepper, cumin, and a little olive oil and lemon juice. Whole fish, steaks or just pieces of fish are smothered in marinade for various lengths of time and usually they are stewed or grilled. It is common for cooks to place fish to be stewed on a matting of thinly sliced or julienned vegetables to prevent it from sticking to the bottom of the dish (see recipes: *tagine bil hut,* p. 60, and *bousaif bil chermula,* p. 61). Another way to prepare marinated fish is to grill it on skewers. As with meat kebabs, the Moroccan method is to put nothing else on the skewer but fish. The beloved *chermula* marinade also flavors fish stuffings. A classic is rice and olives mixed with the marinade.

As a mainstay of the diet, vegetables not surprisingly are also prominent in stews (*tagines*), many of which glorify just vegetables. It is not typical to find vegetables served as "sides." The larder abounds with tomatoes, onions, leeks, garlic, potatoes, eggplants, sweet and hot peppers, okra, turnips, zucchini, chickpeas, beans (fresh and dried), carrots, artichokes (including wild ones), pumpkins, beets, lettuce and mushrooms. Many different combinations are used for inexpensive, vegetarian stews. The common cucumber is a long, slightly ridged variety with less water and fewer seeds than the usual type of cucumber grown in the United States. A long, pale-green, slightly curved squash called *slaoui* makes its most celebrated appearance in the dish called *seksu* Beidaoui, the classic Casablanca-style dish of couscous with seven vegetables (see recipe, p. 51). Special stews feature (and are named for) the wild and domesticated thistles, relatives of the artichoke. *Kanaria* is a saffron-flavored stew containing the domesticated thistle, or cardoon (*Cynara cardunculus*). The *kanaria* stalks are trimmed of leaves, thorns, and tough fibers, cut into small pieces, and cooked along with meat and preserved lemons. A stew of similar composition available only in the spring—*gernina*—contains pale-green stems of the wild thistle, which are notoriously difficult to trim of tough parts. One's labor is rewarded, however,

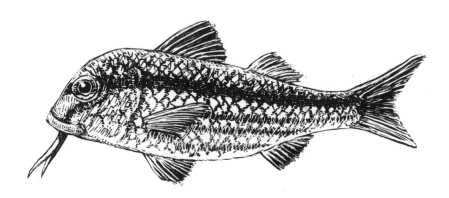

Red mullet, an especially prized catch of the day in Morocco. It is enjoyed grilled over charcoal, baked or cooked in stews. A "dry," highly seasoned marinade called *chermula* is commonly rubbed on the fish before it is cooked.

by the much-prized bitter flavor the stems impart to the stew and the restorative properties they are said to have on liver function.

Other meat and vegetable stews include *lham bil quq wa gra^c taxrifin,* which features globe artichokes and zucchini (see recipe, p. 54), and *tagine lham bil khodra* Fassi, Fès-style lamb with seasonal vegetables (see recipe, p. 53, and photo, color insert). The humble and very satisfying Berber vegetarian dish called *byesar* is a hearty, thick purée of broad (fava) beans topped with some paprika, cumin and a drizzle of oil. It is breakfast street food that resembles hummus, which is made of chickpeas. In Marrakech and the surrounding countryside markets, it typically is cooked in characteristic round-bottomed, earthenware crocks with flared rims. These cooking vessels sit at an angle on a charcoal burner to facilitate removal of their contents with a long-handled ladle.

Salads are refreshing first-course offerings consisting of raw or lightly cooked fresh vegetables sweetened or flavored with spices. They are not the dressed mixture of leafy greens and chopped fresh vegetables familiar to us, although that type of salad may be available in hotels catering specifically to tourists. Uncooked vegetable salads are served cold; cooked ones are eaten warm or cold. Unusual combinations of ingredients surprise and delight the palate. *Khizu bil limun* is a salad of grated carrots and sliced oranges (or just orange-flower water) dusted with cinnamon. *Chakchouka* is a cold tomato and sweet pepper salad. The dish is named after the bubbling sound the mixture makes as it simmers and reduces to a purée without water. Another popular cooked salad is *zahlouk,* made with eggplant and tomato (see recipe, p. 44). *Bakoola* is a salad of sautéed wild greens (see recipes, pp. 42–43). Mallow, a nutritious spinach-like plant with large leaves typically is used, and chard is substituted when mallow is out of season. Other favorite substitutes are spinach and purslane. Fruit salads also are well-liked, particularly one called *shlada limun,* which has overlapping orange slices flavored with orange flower-water and is dusted with cinnamon and sugar (see recipe, p. 46). This pleasing salad makes a good dessert as well.

The soup category is dominated by the beloved *harira* and its many regional variations. This traditional, hearty soup is made with lamb or meatballs, legumes, such as lentils, chickpeas, and fava beans, and tomatoes and onions. It is often flavored with saffron and cilantro (see recipe, p. 41). Just before serving, it is thickened with *tedouira,* a mixture of flour or yeast and water that sometimes is slightly fermented. Beaten eggs can also be added to enrich and thicken the soup. *Harira* is enjoyed year-round, but invariably is served at sundown each day during the month-long fast of Ramadan when no food or drink can be taken between sunrise and sunset. *Harira* is eaten with a ladle-like, hand-carved spoon called a *mgerfa* (*mgorfa*) made from lemon or orange wood shown on p. 10. Typical soup accompaniments are dates or sweet pastries called *shebbakiya*, which resemble irregular coils of ribbons. *Harira kerwiya* is a lemon-flavored mint and caraway soup that traditionally is served with lamb's head in the morning. A light soup without flour, egg or yeast thickeners is called *chorba*. It sometimes has large-grained couscous (*mhammsa*) in it. Examples include *chorba bil dshisha*, which is made with crushed grains of wheat; *chorba bil ful*, a Passover soup of fava beans flavored with cilantro that is on the Moroccan Jewish menu; and *chorba bil khodra*, a vegetable soup flavored with saffron.

Fruits flourish in Morocco. Market vendors keep a bit of the stem and a leaf or two on the fruit to indicate how recently it was picked. A platter of fresh, seasonal fruit ends a Moroccan meal, and gives diners much to enjoy. The citrus family includes plump oranges, lemons, limes and the favored tangerine, a variety of mandarin orange named for Tangier. Also abundant in season are pears, peaches, apples, mangoes, figs, dates, cherries, plums, bananas, quinces, grapes, melons, mulberries, tiny pale apricots, huge strawberries and the Barbary fig (the spiny fruit of the prickly pear cactus). Many of the fruits are dried and used in savory and sweet dishes and, as such, are a nice complement to the spices. Almonds and walnuts are plentiful. Used ground, chopped or whole, they add interesting texture to a great variety of sweet and savory dishes.

Highlights of Moroccan dairy products are yogurt and an interesting mix of fine French-style cheeses and the indigenous farmer's cheese. *Raipe* is a type of yogurt made from milk thickened by the bristly "chokes" (or "beards") of certain artichokes or thistles. If the mixture sits for a day and then is put into a cheesecloth bag and squeezed to remove the moisture, a soft farmer's cheese (*jben*) is obtained. If the mixture rests for three to four days before being squeezed, a harder cheese called *iklil* is made. Addition of salt extends the shelf-life of the cheese. The choke from a type of artichoke (*Cynara humilis*) or cardoon (domesticated thistle, *Cynara cardunculus*) contains rennets that curdle milk to produce cheese. Connoisseurs prefer the taste of cheese produced by the chokes of *Cynara humilis*. Before the chokes are added to milk, they are pounded into a paste, or dried and pulverized. Fresh buttermilk (*lben*) is made from naturally curdled fresh milk and enjoyed especially with *seffa*, a sweet dessert made with couscous.

As in many cultures, the importance of bread (*khobz*) in Morocco is evident in the reverence held for it. Classic, crusty, round loaves, traditionally leavened and flat, are about eight to ten inches wide, one to two inches thick, and very absorbent. Aniseed and sesame seeds frequently are added for flavoring, particularly in breads made for special occasions. Cut wedges or torn pieces of bread are held with the fingers of the right hand as utensils to pick up food. Since most homes do not have an oven, bread is baked in a large communal oven. Unbaked loaves prepared at home are given an identification mark, placed on a wooden board and covered with a cloth. Children typically transport the loaves to the oven and back. Another type of bread to savor is *harsha,* large circular sheets (about 15 inches in diameter) of flat, unleavened Berber bread made of course semolina flour. Street vendors cut it into pieces and do a brisk business in the morning. *Khobz meqli* is a grainy, fried flatbread made with semolina flour (see recipe, p. 46). Travelers are less apt to come across the curved Berber loaf of leavened flatbread called *tunnert*. Pizza-like circular slabs of dough are slapped onto the inside wall of a round earthen oven that is open on one side and vented on top. Loaves are baked until crispy, and when removed from the oven, they retain the curvature of the wall.

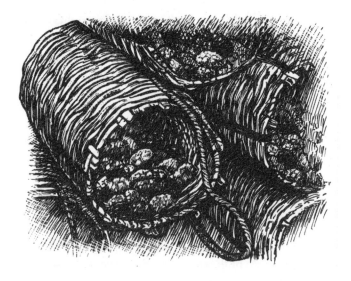

Mulberries for sale in the medina in Fès. Tall, round baskets (*ferx*) with handles are used to transport and sell the succulent berries.

Morocco's culinary repertoire includes a group of sweet and savory dishes made with ultrathin—and in some hands almost transparent—sheets of pastry made of small, overlapping circles of dough. Unlike the classic ultrathin rolled or stretched doughs of Turkey (*yufka*) and Greece (*phyllo*), a sheet of *warka* is made by taking a ball of dough about the size of a tennis ball and tapping it repeatedly on a heated round metal pan (*tobsil dial warka*) until the entire surface of the pan is covered. Each tap leaves a small circle of dough on the pan, and by having each small circle slightly overlap the adjacent one, a sheet the size of the pan is produced. The dough cooks quickly and is carefully lifted off the surface of the pan. (See color insert for photos of *warka* being made.) Several sheets are used to make the crowning glory of Morocco's kitchen, the classic squab pie called *bestila*.

To make *bestila,* the squab (or chicken, which is sometimes substituted) is cooked whole in a sauce that includes onion, pepper, parsley, saffron, cinnamon and sugar. When done, it is removed from the pan, cut into pieces, usually without boning, and put on top of a few layers of pastry placed on a special round, shallow-rimmed cooking pan (*tobsil dial bestila*). The pastry needs to extend considerably beyond the edges of the pan to provide for adequate sealing of the pie during the last steps of its assembly. To achieve this, several single pastry circles are overlapped to form a composite layer that is larger than the pan. The highly seasoned meat layer is covered with more pastry and topped with eggs that have been scrambled in the reduced sauce the meat cooked in plus some lemon juice. Additional pastry is placed over this and covered with a mixture of ground, toasted almonds, cinnamon and granulated sugar that has been pounded to a fine powder. After this step, the pastry extending beyond the pan is brought up and folded over the top of the pie before the final pastry layer is added and its edges tucked way underneath to enclose the entire pie. After the *bestila* is baked, powdered sugar is sprinkled on top and a geometric design is drawn on top of that with cinnamon.

Briwat and *brik* are other classic pastries using *warka*. *Briwat* are small, plump triangles made of *warka* that is wrapped around sweet or savory fillings. To make *briwat,* a spoonful of filling is placed near one end of a strip of lightly oiled pastry. Either corner of the pastry where the filling was placed is picked up and put over the filling. This triangle-shaped portion is then raised and folded over onto the adjacent part of the pastry sheet, maintaining the triangular shape in the process. The triangle continues to fatten as it is folded back and forth until the end of the pastry sheet has been reached. Any loose ends are tucked inside before the pastry is baked or deep-fried. *Briwat* can also be rectangular or cigar-shaped. *Brik* is a savory filled pastry of Tunisian origin similar to the *briwat*. The filling typically contains eggs with cilantro and parsley, and often is spiked with a little *harissa,* a hot red paste made from chile peppers. The pastry must be eaten immediately after it is fried, and the egg should remain runny.

Thin crêpe-like pastry is used to create the dish called *trid*, which is considered a primitive form of *bestila*. The dough is oily because it contains vegetable oil in addition to flour and water. It is divided into small balls about the size of an egg, and kept moist with more oil. Each ball of dough is stretched and tugged by well-oiled hands on a board or some other hard surface, to make a circle of the desired size and thickness. The sheets are then baked on a heated, dome-like utensil called a *gedra dial trid.* The dish is assembled by layering baked sheets in a *tagine* with sauce from a mixture of saffron- and ginger-flavored chicken in between the pastry layers. The chicken and remaining sauce are put on top of the stack and garnished with toasted almonds.

Another special dough-based item to try is *beghrir,* a yeast-raised semolina pancake cooked on one side only, without oil, in a round, unglazed earthenware dish. The "uncooked," upper side is full of little holes. The pancake traditionally is enjoyed for breakfast, and more recently, as a dessert, with melted butter and honey or sugar.

A family of flat breakfast pastries collectively called *rghaif* are made with yeast-raised dough. These pastries generally are eaten with butter and honey. The dough is rolled thin, folded into various shapes and fried. Oil or melted butter, and sometimes sweet or savory fillings, are spread on the surface of the dough before folds are made. A favorite filling is *khlii,* sun-dried, spice-cured strips of beef. Dough can also be drawn out into threads and wound into bundles that are pressed flat and fried. *Melowi* is a type of *rghaif* made by taking a thin rectangle of dough, rolling it up like a jellyroll, standing the roll up on one end and squashing the whole thing flat. The pastry is then fried. *Roztel kadi* is a version named "judge's turban" because of its appearance. The dough is rolled into a fine thread and coiled to make a flat, circular pastry that is fried. *Mtsimen* is made by folding dough into a wedge and griddle-frying it. *Wadnine el kadi* is a folded and fried pastry named the "judge's ears." It is formed by taking a small ball of dough and rolling it into a very thin square, which is then folded into thirds by bringing first one side then the other over the middle section. This process is repeated after rotating the strip 90 degrees, producing a square pastry about 4–5 inches wide and nine layers thick. Before it is fried, the pastry square is stretched on each of its four sides to produce uneven contours.

Searches for the derivation of food names frequently uncover interesting stories. This charming tale of old, told by Souad, our guide in Marrakech, recounts how this type of *rghaif* came to be called *wadnine el kadi,* or "judges ears." The explanation involves a learned judge with huge ears and his trusted barber. The judge was so ashamed of his ears that he hid their enormity in the folds of a large turban, which only was taken off when a haircut was needed. The barber alone knew the judge's secret, but was unable to keep his silence forever. One day he walked into a grove of trees and told a sapling about the judge's deformity. The barber was greatly relieved to be able to release his secret, even if only to a small tree. Years passed. One day the tree was felled and a maker of musical instruments obtained the wood. As if magically, the beautiful instruments cut from the wood could play no music, and repeatedly whispered these words instead, "The judge has big ears." News of this rapidly reached the judge, who was so enraged that he called for the immediate death of the barber. Calmer individuals, however, were able to prevail upon the judge to spare the barber. They convinced him that it was his very ears that made him so acclaimed. They allowed that since the judge's ears could hear so well in all directions simultaneously, he was capable of greater wisdom than those with ordinary ears! And thus the barber lived to cut more hair, and the judge no longer hid his ears. So, when you are in Morocco, have *wadnine el kadi* for breakfast some day, and enjoy a good laugh when you observe the shape of it.

Moroccan kitchens produce numerous spectacular sweet treats, but they are meant for special occasions or are destined for the tea table, not for dessert (see photo, color insert). The usual ending to a Moroccan meal is mint tea and a platter of fresh fruit. Nevertheless, pastries and other sweets are on menus, and travelers are able to enjoy them as desserts. Pastry shops also are full of temptations for the sweet tooth.

Almond paste is a common ingredient of pastries, many of which make use of the ultrathin sheets of *warka*. Honey-soaked pastry triangles made with *warka* and filled with almond paste, *briwat bil luz,* are addictive (see recipe, p. 62). M'hanncha, "the snake," is a real show stopper. It is a tight coil of pastry stuffed with almond paste, baked until golden, dusted with powdered sugar and decorated with lines drawn with cinnamon. To make *m'hanncha,* sheets of *warka* are wrapped around long "sausages" of almond paste that has been flavored with orange-flower water. These wrapped lengths of pastry-encased almond paste are then arranged in a tight coil, beginning at the center of a round baking pan. Several lengths are needed to complete the coil. *Kaᶜb el ghzal* are crescent-shaped pastries called "gazelle's horns," which are filled with almond paste (see illustration, p. 13, and recipe, p. 64). Only a very thin shell of pastry (not *warka*) encases the filling. Orange-flower water is added to the dough and often to the almond paste as well. A type of "gazelle's horns" dipped in orange-flower water and coated with powdered sugar is called *kaᶜb el ghzal m'fenned*.

Several cookies are national favorites. *Ghoriba* is a rich, buttery semolina cookie with a crinkled, macaroon-like surface dusted with powdered sugar (see recipe, p. 66). Some versions are made with regular flour and are more like shortbread. Crushed, toasted sesame seeds or finely minced almonds can be added to the dough. *Feqqas* are twice-baked, biscotti-like cookies flavored with anise and sesame seeds (see recipe, p. 65). Raisins and almonds are often

Sfinge, yeast-raised doughnuts typically eaten in the morning. They are a popular street food enjoyed with mint tea. Vendors deftly form the doughnuts by hand and deep-fry them in a large vat of hot oil. If the doughnuts are carried away to be eaten elsewhere, they are transported on a strip cut from a palm leaf and tied in a loop, as shown. Coarsely pounded sugar is sprinkled over the doughnuts before they are eaten.

added. To make them, quarter-inch-thick rounds are cut from a partially baked cylinder of dough and baked again.

For pudding lovers, *ruz bil hleb* is a tasty comfort food of creamy rice pudding flavored with orange-flower water. This velvety dish is delicious hot or cold.

Tea is Morocco's passion. Many glasses of the national drink are enjoyed at the end of a meal, and throughout the day. There is an entrenched social ritual associated with brewing and serving tea. One must have a *siniya,* an often ornate three-footed tray, to hold everything needed to make the beverage: a pot-bellied teapot (*berrad*), tea glasses, and boxes containing Chinese green tea, loaf sugar and fresh spearmint. The master of the house brews and serves the tea. At several points while the tea is steeping, he pours out a small amount into a glass and tastes it. More sugar will be added if it is not sweet enough. When the tea is judged ready, the teapot is raised high above the glasses on the tray, and the tea is carefully and dramatically poured (see photo, color insert). One must wait for the glasses to cool a bit before drinking. One no longer feels obligated to drink three glasses of tea at a sitting, as social protocol once dictated.

Coffee is a distant second to tea. Moroccans like Turkish-style coffee and appreciate it best when it is strong, sweet and flavored with orange-flower water. Fresh fruit juices are plentiful and perennially pleasing. Of them, pomegranate, orange and lemon juices are traditional, and a dash of orange-flower water or cinnamon sometimes is added to heighten the flavor. Fruit or nut-milk drinks (*sharbat*) of Egyptian origin are served to celebrate joyful events. Especially tasty and refreshing is *sharbat bil luz,* an almond-flavored milk drink. It should come as no surprise that non-traditional soft drinks, and Coca-Cola in particular, have become ubiquitous around the country. Good drinking water is readily available. Brands of non-carbonated bottled mineral water are Sidi Ali, Sidi Harazem and Imouzzer. Oulmes is a brand of carbonated bottled mineral water. As a joke, tap water is called Sidi Robinet, after the French word for tap water, *robinet.*

Alcohol is readily available in Morocco, although Muslims are forbidden to drink it. Wine actually has been made in Morocco since Roman times, but today's product follows in the rich tradition of French winemaking, a legacy of the French occupancy in the 20th century. Among the impressive wines are those that come from the region around Meknès in the foothills of the Atlas Mountains. A fine beer, "Casablanca," is brewed and bottled in Casablanca.

The Regions of Morocco

Four major, rugged mountain chains carve Morocco into three geographic regions. Much of the country lies at high elevation. The interior is dominated by the Rif Mountains in the north and a series of three, distinct Atlas Mountain ranges—the nation's rocky backbone—that overlap and slash diagonally across the region on a roughly northeast–southwest axis. The Rif Mountain chain forms a crescent along the Mediterranean, with cliffs sometimes dropping precipitously to the sea. Few harbors exist along the rugged coastline. The highest peaks of the Rifs reach about 8,000 feet above sea level. The narrow Taza Gap separates this mountain chain from the Middle Atlas, the northernmost of the three Atlas ranges, which has peaks reaching an altitude of about 11,000 feet. The High Atlas is the loftiest and longest of the three ranges, beginning as low hills near the Atlantic, south of and approximately parallel to the Middle Atlas range. The highest peak of the Atlas Mountains, and in North Africa as well, is Mount Toubkal at about 13,500 feet, south of Marrakech. Farthest south is the Anti Atlas range, running south of the High Atlas, and lying in the desert borderlands. Its peaks reach little more than 7,800 feet. Between the Atlas Mountains and the Atlantic Ocean is the coastal lowland region, insulated from the Sahara by the Atlas Mountains. The arid region is southeast and south of the Atlas Mountains, and includes pre-Saharan Morocco and the northwestern limit of the Sahara Desert.

The Coastal Plains

The fertile coastal region includes the Rharb (Gharb), Chaouia, Doukkala, Meseta, Abda, Tadla and Haouz plains. Practically all of the nation's modern commercial agriculture is centered here. Several different crops are cultivated: grains, such as wheat, barley, corn and rice; legumes, such as chickpeas, broad beans, peas and lentils; sugarcane, sugar beets, grapes, olives; potatoes, tomatoes, onions, carrots and many other seasonal vegetables. Greenhouse gardening is extensive. The rich lowland area of the north, the Rharb plain, is a major fruit-growing area, with an emphasis on citrus fruits. Oranges and tangerines make up the bulk of the harvest, and a sizable quantity is exported. Tobacco, tea and soybeans are more recent crops that have fared well in the fertile Rharb plain. In some areas there is extensive growth of the Barbary fig (prickly pear cactus), whose fruit is dried and sold in the *souks*. The plants grow in long, single rows, like fences, over miles of the countryside.

Lifestock raising is widespread. Cows, sheep and goats, some of which are tethered, are patiently tended by rural families in the fields near their homes.

Most Moroccans—more than 75 percent of the country's population—inhabit the Atlantic coastal plain. Almost all the large cities and towns are located in this region. Prominent cities include Tangier, Casablanca, the largest city and main port; Rabat, the capital, Fès, Meknès, and Marrakech in the south, at the foothills of the High Atlas. The cities of Agadir and Essaouira (Mogador) are popular tourist destinations on the Atlantic in the south.

Along Morocco's Atlantic coast, the cold waters of the Canaries Current ensure an abundant supply of fish, and restaurants in coastal ports from Tangier to Tan-Tan have reason to flaunt it on their menus. In Essaouira, fish lovers can await the returning fleet and get their choice cooked on one of many open-air grills. A specialty of Oualidia, a small fishing village south of Casablanca, is *seksu bil hut,* a dish of couscous topped with vegetables and served with fish fillets and mussels around the edge of the platter. *Hut b'noua*—saffron-flavored baked fish, stuffed and topped with almond paste—is an offering in Safi. Almond paste is also used as a stuffing for chicken here. Another fish stuffing used in Safi is saffron-flavored rice. Stuffed sardines are common street food in Safi, whereas fish stews made with sardines are characteristic of Tetouan.

Several of Morocco's rivers have been dammed to provide water for irrigation, since the extent of rainfall fluctuates sharply. Although irrigation has improved agriculture in Morocco, the dams have the unintended consequence of increasing the salinity of downstream river estuaries, which jeopardizes the habitat of fish and other wildlife. The shad, one of Morocco's favorite food fish, is becoming a rarity because of the double threat of overfishing and habitat loss.

Many consider Fès to be the culinary center of Morocco. Several classic dishes are associated with this city. Among the stews made in Fès are two using some unusual vegetables available in the area. *Kanaria (qennariya)* contains stalks of the domesticated thistle plant, and *gernina (garnina)* has pale-green stems of wild thistles. Small, wild artichokes make an early appearance in the spring and the hearts are a tasty addition to meat dishes. *Tagine m'derbel* is a famous lamb stew topped with a purée of either pumpkin or eggplant. The vegetables are sliced, salted, dried and then cooked in oil until they become puréed. Saffron-flavored chicken cooked in sauce with *smen* (aged butter) is also a regional specialty. The Fassi (people from Fès) make an Andalusian-style lamb dish (*tagine lham tafaya*) flavored with saffron and ginger that is topped with quartered hard-boiled eggs and toasted, blanched almonds. Another lamb dish of the same name, a national favorite, has a sweet topping of red onions, raisins, almonds and honey flavored with saffron, cinnamon and rose water. An area specialty featuring squab is a preparation using almonds in a savory stuffing (*frach m^cammar bil luz*). A tomato purée or jam sweetened with honey (*matisha m'sla*) is used as a sauce with meat or as a preserve (see recipe, p. 45). Sweets found in Fès include *jaban*, a nougat-like candy. Vendors in the souks of the medina display large blocks of *jaban*, which they cut into slices. Sweet tooths may also want to search for some *helwa jenjlan*, blocks of caramelized sugar full of sesame seeds.

The regal *keneffa*, a sweet dessert version of *bestila* (the classic squab pie), is a specialty of Marrakech. Between the pastry layers is a thickened almond-milk mixture flavored with orange-flower water, which is covered with coarsely chopped almonds coated with cinnamon and sugar. The top pastry layer is decorated with powdered sugar and stripes of cinnamon. Another dish associated with Marrakech is *tangia* Mrakchiya, or bachelor's stew. It is a one-dish meal made of well-seasoned meat and onions that is placed in a two-handled earthenware crock or amphora—also called a *tangia*—and slowly cooked for hours on embers in a public oven. Some of the best *mechoui* is sold in stalls just off the famous square in the medina, Jemaa el Fna, in Marrakech. Mechoui is whole-cooked lamb spit-roasted over hot embers for several hours and basted frequently with butter seasoned with garlic, cumin and paprika. It will not be difficult to choose the best meat, because the stall selling it will be the busiest. Spicy, Marrakech-style kebabs, *quodban* Mrakchiya, are served in pockets of warmed bread, with a pinch of cumin, some tomato and onion relish and a spoonful of *harissa*, the thick, spicy condiment made with dried hot red chile peppers, olive oil and garlic. Marrakech is also noted for *tagine sferjel*, a sweet stew of lamb and quinces.

One of the ubiquitous dishes available to travelers takes its name from the Arabic for Casablanca, Dar-el-Beida (white house). *Seksu* Beidaoui is the tasty dish of couscous with seven vegetables (see recipe, p. 51). A dish enjoyed in Rabat is *djaj tarat*, a vegetable platter of potatoes, chickpeas and onions, flavored with *smen* (aged butter), saffron and cilantro. It is cooked until just a light sauce is left, and served in individual dishes. There is no chicken (*djaj*) in this preparation, despite its name. It is said that the fowl meant for the stew pot got away and that is how *djaj tarat* became a vegetarian offering. Nearby Sale's specialty stew is *tagine* Slaoui *bil kefta*, a dish of meatballs in a spicy tomato sauce. *Kamama* is a specialty of Meknès. This sweet lamb stew is seasoned with ginger and topped with saffron- and cinnamon-flavored onion rings that have cooked in *smen* and olive oil.

Essaouira is known for several Jewish dishes. The city once was home to the biggest Jewish quarter (*melha*) in Morocco. Few Jews remain in Morocco today, but their dishes are a lasting legacy. *Djaj k'dra touimiya* is a preparation of chicken with chickpeas and almonds in a buttery sauce with onions, pepper and saffron. The twin (*touimiya*) foods are chickpeas and almonds, two classic ingredients of Moorish Spain, home of the forebears of many Moroccan Jews before the Reconquest in 1492. The Jewish fondness for beef and veal is reflected in the dish *tagine lham d-le-ᶜjel bil zitun wa batata,* a garlic-

Tangia Mrakchiya, or "bachelor's stew," is a specialty of Marrakech. It is a one-dish meal made of well-seasoned meat and onions that is placed in a two-handled earthenware crock or amphora—also called a *tangia*—and slowly cooked for hours on embers in a public oven.

flavored veal stew with olives and potatoes. Chicken dishes include *djaj bil hamus,* chicken and chickpeas flavored with turmeric and cumin, and *djaj bil gra^c taxrifin,* chicken and zucchini in an oniony sauce (see recipe, p. 54). Fish balls poached in a spicy tomato sauce are a perennial favorite, as are *briwat (briouat),* small, plump triangles made of thin sheets of pastry dough *(warka)* wrapped around a savory filling of fish. A Jewish specialty associated with Tangier is an especially sweet dish of couscous with meatballs, pumpkin, prunes and cinnamon, which is often served for special occasions.

The Mountain Highlands

The Rif and Atlas Mountains are home to about 20 percent of the country's population. The Rif Mountains in the north enjoy a Mediterranean climate and the most rainfall of Morocco's ranges. The region is inhabited primarily by the Rifi Berbers, who are mostly farming people. The Berbers built terraces on the mountain slopes to increase the acreage suitable for growing their crops, which include seasonal vegetables, legumes, and grains, such as corn, sorghum, wheat and barley. Much of their income is derived from the sale of nuts and fruits. Cash crops include almonds and walnuts, and a variety of fruits, such as plums, apricots, apples, cherries, figs and olives. Sardine fishing is also important. Herds of sheep and goats are raised on grazing grounds in the mountains during the summer months. The milk is used to make *jben,* the indigenous Moroccan farmer's cheese. It can be a soft, spreadable cheese of uniform consistency or firmer with small cavities. Berber farmer's cheese made in the Rif Mountains is salted and often sold at the markets in small, round, shallow baskets by Rifi women in traditional attire. Their bright, vertically striped skirts and shawls, and festive, wide-brimmed straw hats with colored pom-poms made of yarn are spectacular.

Nestled in a fold of the mountains is the captivating town of Chaouen (or Chefchaouen), whose medina showcases many old Andalusian-style buildings whitewashed a light powder blue. It was settled primarily by refugees from Moorish Spain in the 15th century. Specialties of the area include a fish stew made with sardines and Chaouen-style couscous *(seksu),* a plate of couscous with a hefty mound of chickpeas and honeyed raisins on top (see photo, color insert). Another local variant of the ever-popular Moroccan stew contains red mullet, fava beans and raisins and is flavored with saffron. A chicken specialty is *djaj bil berquq,* chicken with prunes. Tetouan, another city with

Andalusian heritage, is in the foothills of the Rif. It is known for several vegetarian stews, including *marak matisha bil mlokhia,* a stew of tomatoes and okra.

A large part of the Rif centered around Ketama is devoted to the growth of marijuana. Travelers who don't want to be framed for drug-trafficking would be wise to find out ahead of time which areas pose risks.

The Atlas Mountains cover about a third of Morocco. Their northern slopes are well-watered in comparison to their arid southern ones. Moisture-laden winds from the Atlantic bring rainfall, which is most plentiful in the north and decreases southward. Streams are fed by slow-melting snow caps of the High Atlas.

The Atlas ranges are populated by several different Berber tribes. Many are semi-nomadic. Their economy is based on raising livestock, and is dependent on the seasonal transfer of grazing herds, alternating between mountain highlands and lowland plains, depending on the growing season. Some tribe members forego the migrations and remain year round in their permanent villages on mountain slopes and high plateaus in order to tend terraced gardens and fortified community granaries (*agadir*). Seasonal crops include vegetables, wheat, barley, corn, millet, and rye. Also grown are blackberries, mint and grapes. Almond, walnut and pomegranate trees are cultivated in scattered plots, and at lower elevations, olives and carob trees are also grown.

Since the selection of dishes in Morocco's restaurants is fairly limited, travelers will need to visit *souks* (markets) or homes to sample some of the staples of Berber cuisine. One such dish is *dshisha,* a seasoned porridge or couscous prepared with wheat or barley grits topped with a medley of vegetables, and perhaps some chicken. A type of couscous made with cornmeal is called *dshisha dial dra.* Boiled greens are chopped and mixed with the couscous. The dish also can contain meat. Other names for *dshisha dial dra* are *dshisha belbula* and *baddaz.* Yet another variation is *dshisha sikuk,* made with barley grits and fava beans. A dish of barley couscous with turnips and carrots, *seksu belbula,* is a traditional favorite. *Byesar* is a hearty, thick, Berber dish of puréed broad (fava) beans topped with some paprika, cumin and a drizzle of oil. It resembles hummus, which is made of chickpeas. Homemade Berber sausage is called *ikerdasen* (or *kurbass*). Several types of meat are rubbed with a mixture of coriander, white pepper, paprika, cumin, saffron and salt, and dried in the sun for a few days. The meat is then chopped into small pieces, seasoned with more of the spice, and stuffed into casings.

The Souss River valley in southwestern Morocco, situated between the High Atlas and Anti Atlas mountain ranges, is the habitat of the indigenous *argan* tree (*Argania sideroxylon, Argania spinosa*). The tree grows nowhere else in the world. It is extremely well adapted to drought and poor soils, and appears to be an ancient relic species. The fruit of the *argan* tree is the source of a nutritious, nutty-flavored, edible oil (*zit argan*), which is a rich, rusty orange color. Using artisanal methods, Berbers in the area have been extracting oil from the seeds for centuries. They arduously knead by hand a mixture of roasted, ground seeds and warm water. After a rinse with more water, the oil floating on the surface is removed. Produced this way, *argan* oil is relatively perishable. The modern, waterless, cold-pressed extraction method results in a more stable product. See *Resources,* p. 71, for a mail-order source of organic, cold-pressed *argan* oil in the United States.

Exotic, toasted *argan* oil is a flavorful, much-prized substitute for olive oil in southwestern Morocco. It is mixed with almonds to make an almond butter called *amlou* (see recipe, p. 67), and also is used in making pastries and

Goat on a branch of the thorny argan tree (*Argania sideroxylon*) native to southwestern Morocco. Its fruit is the source of a nutty-flavored, edible oil used in this region. The goats that climb up the trees to feed on the fruit's flesh provide tourists with a spectacular photo opportunity.

for dipping bread. Chefs around the world are beginning to discover its merits and are creating dishes to showcase it.

Argan fruits also provide food for goats, which climb up the trees to nibble the flesh off the nut. Travelers are amused to see trees along the roadside filled with feeding goats. Clever goat herders keep their flocks close to the highways and augment their income with tips from tourists who like to stop and take pictures of the goats in the trees.

Many crops are grown in the fertile Souss basin, including tomatoes, bananas, oranges, olives, barley, corn and apples. Almonds are grown at higher elevations up the mountain slopes. The area around Agadir is famous for its honey. Bee-keeping is one of the principal activities of the region, and a festival celebrating honey is held early in May in the small village of Immouzzer des Ida Outanane. A popular dish in the Souss is *casidah,* a thick soup or porridge made from barley grits. It is formed into balls and eaten with butter and honey.

Saffron grows in the countryside around the town of Taliouine, which is located near the east end of the fertile Souss basin. Travelers are welcome to visit the saffron cooperative in town. The organization maintains a small museum with posters (in French) explaining their product. Packets of excellent quality spice can be purchased inexpensively there.

The Arid Lands

Rolling plateaus east of the Atlas Mountains receive very little rain, and nothing more than scrub grows there. Farther south is the hammada, a flat or undulating, pre-Saharan tract of barren land covered with stone fragments. The hammada gradually gives way to the desert of southeastern and southern Morocco.

Relatively few Moroccans live in this arid region. Inhabited areas are oasis settlements with lush palm groves lining the river beds. Dates are cultivated as a cash crop, and grains, vegetables and fruit trees are grown in small plots beneath the date palm fronds. Water for irrigation and domestic use is provided by rivers from the southeastern side of the Atlas Mountains—if the waterways have not dried up or abruptly disappeared beneath the surface— or is tapped from underground mountain water sources. A well is dug to locate this underground water, typically to a depth of several hundred feet beneath the sand dunes and uphill from the land where water is needed.

Since a good well often is far from the irrigation site, an ingenious underground *qanat,* or series of tunnels, is dug to link the two. Within the buried tunnels an artificial river flows downhill from the well. In some instances, water is brought in this manner over distances of several hundred miles.

In an oasis, dwellings typically are at the periphery of the irrigated land. Many inhabitants live in old, high-walled fortified villages, *ksour* (singular *ksar*), which usually have impressive, decorated towers. These structures typically are built of mud and wattle from palm trees. The bigger villages have a central square, living quarters to accommodate many families, mosques, shops, and communal ovens to bake bread. The black inhabitants of oases are called Harratin, thought by some to be descendants of ancient aboriginal peoples.

Stews featuring dates, such as the lamb stew *lham bil tmer,* attest to the popularity of this vital commodity. A recipe for chicken with dates, *djaj bil tmer,* is provided (see p. 58). Dates are enjoyed out of hand, as a topping for salads, and stuffed with a variety of fillings, such as almond paste. Sometimes the paste is tinted green with food coloring because green is said to have been the favorite color of the Prophet Mohammed. Dates are also a common addition to the fruit platter served at the end of a Moroccan meal. Travelers visiting the town of Erfoud in the Tafilalt Oasis during the October date harvest can enjoy an annual festival celebrating the event. A favorite soup or breakfast porridge in the Tifilalt area is *felalia.* This thick, light-yellow cooked cereal is made with barley and laced with thin strips cut from leaves of a wild plant.

Camels are raised for meat in the Sahara and some *souks* have it for sale. Stews with camel (*tagine lham jmel*) are available for interested travelers.

Tastes of Morocco

You are encouraged to try some of these classic and nouvelle Moroccan recipes before you leave home. This is a wonderful and immediately rewarding way to preview the extraordinary cuisine of Morocco. Most of the special Moroccan ingredients necessary for these recipes are available in the United States (see *Resources,* p. 71). Satisfactory substitutes are given for those that are unavailable.

SOUPS

Harira

Peppery meat, vegetable and legume soup. Serves 8–10.

The recipe for this traditional soup, which breaks the fast during Ramadan, was provided by Rafih and Rita Benjelloun, co-owners of The Imperial Fez, the popular and acclaimed Moroccan restaurant in Atlanta, Georgia. Rafih is from Fès, the oldest Imperial city of Morocco, and Rita is from Marrakech, one of the most popular tourist destinations in Morocco.

> ¼ CUP CHICKPEAS (SOAKED IN WATER 24 HOURS)
>
> ¼ CUP FAVA BEANS (SOAKED IN WATER 24 HOURS AND SKINNED)
>
> ¼ CUP LENTILS
>
> SALT TO TASTE
>
> ¼ CUP OLIVE OIL
>
> 1 LARGE ONION, FINELY CHOPPED
>
> ½ POUND LAMB SHOULDER, DICED INTO ½-INCH PIECES
>
> 1 POUND TOMATOES, SEEDED AND PUREED (ABOUT 1 CUP)
>
> ½ CUP TOMATO PASTE
>
> ½ CUP FRESH CILANTRO, FINELY CHOPPED
>
> ½ CUP FRESH FLAT-LEAF PARSLEY, FINELY CHOPPED
>
> 2 TABLESPOONS BLACK PEPPER

[Harira, *continued*]

> 2 TABLESPOONS CUMIN
>
> 1 TABLESPOON CORIANDER
>
> 3 BAY LEAVES
>
> 10–15 CUPS WATER
>
> SALT TO TASTE
>
> 2 CINNAMON STICKS (OPTIONAL)
>
> 4 SPRIGS FRESH SPEARMINT (OPTIONAL)
>
> 3 TABLESPOONS WHOLE-WHEAT FLOUR
>
> ½ CUP WATER

Add chickpeas and fava beans to a pot with 2 cups water and salt to taste. Cook, covered, over medium heat until tender, about 1–1½ hours. Add lentils and cook 10–15 minutes more. Drain and set aside. Heat oil in a large, heavy pot. Add onion and lamb, and sauté until onion is tender. Add tomato purée and paste, cilantro, parsley, pepper, cumin, coriander, bay leaves, water and salt to taste. Add cinnamon sticks and spearmint, if desired. Stir well. Cook over medium-high heat for 20 minutes. Add legumes and cook an additional 10 minutes. Put flour in a small, deep bowl. Gradually add ½ cup water, whisking continuously until well-mixed. Dribble flour mixture into soup, stirring constantly. Cook for 3–5 minutes more. Serve hot.

SALADS

Bakoola bil Zitun

Purée of leafy greens and herbs with olives. Serves 6.

This recipe was provided by Paula Wolfert, whose seminal cookbook on Moroccan food, *Couscous and Other Good Food from Morocco,* published in 1973, was instrumental in bringing authentic Moroccan cookery to a wide audience.

> 4 LARGE CLOVES GARLIC, PEELED
>
> 1 POUND SPINACH, COARSELY CHOPPED (DISCARD STEMS)*
>
> ½ CUP FLAT-LEAF PARSLEY, COARSELY CHOPPED (DISCARD STEMS)
>
> ½ CUP CELERY LEAVES, COARSELY CHOPPED
>
> ½ CUP CILANTRO LEAVES, COARSELY CHOPPED
>
> 4 TABLESPOONS EXTRA-VIRGIN OLIVE OIL
>
> ¼ CUP OIL-CURED OLIVES, PITTED AND COARSELY CHOPPED†
>
> 1¼ TEASPOONS SWEET PAPRIKA OR SMOKY *PIMENTON*††

PINCH CAYENNE PEPPER

PINCH GROUND CUMIN

1 TABLESPOON FRESH LEMON JUICE

SALT AND FRESHLY GROUND BLACK PEPPER TO TASTE

Put garlic cloves in a large steamer basket set over a pan of simmering water and top with spinach, parsley, celery and cilantro. Cover and steam until garlic is soft and greens are very tender, about 15 minutes. Let cool, then squeeze greens dry and transfer to a medium bowl. Using the back of a fork, mash garlic cloves.

In a medium frying pan, heat 1 tablespoon olive oil until shimmering. Add mashed garlic, olives, paprika, cayenne and cumin, and stir over moderately high heat for 30 seconds or until fragrant. Add greens and cook, stirring, until dry, about 2 minutes. Transfer the greens to a medium bowl and let cool to room temperature. Stir in the lemon juice and remaining 3 tablespoons olive oil. Season with salt and black pepper, and serve warm or at room temperature as a salad or as a topping on bread, such as bruschetta. The mixture can be refrigerated for up to 2 days.

*This recipe uses spinach as a substitute for wild greens (*bakoola*). In Morocco this dish is commonly made with a wild, spinach-like plant (mallow) with large leaves. Chard can be substituted for mallow out of season (see following recipe). Another popular mallow substitute is purslane.

†Available at specialty food shops and stores carrying North African and Middle Eastern foods; also see *Resources,* p. 71, for mail-order sources of Moroccan foods.
††*Pimentón*, or Spanish paprika, is available in many varieties, from sweet to smoky. It is available at specialty food shops and Spanish markets.

Bakoola bil Hamd Marked wa Zitun

Cooked greens with preserved lemons and olives. Serves 4.

This recipe was provided by Mustapha Haddouch, owner of Haddouch Gourmet Imports in Seattle. Haddouch imports a variety of Moroccan food products, including olive oil, preserved lemons and an amazing assortment of marinated olives. This cooked salad, a favorite of Mustapha's family, is one often craved by Moroccans traveling abroad.

1½ POUNDS FRESH SWISS CHARD*

1 SMALL PRESERVED LEMON†

2 TABLESPOONS OLIVE OIL

1 TABLESPOON SWEET PAPRIKA

1 TABLESPOON CUMIN

1 TABLESPOON PEPPER

[Bakoola bil Hamd Marked wa Zitun, *continued*]

> 3 TABLESPOONS FRESH CILANTRO, MINCED
>
> 3 TABLESPOONS FRESH FLAT-LEAF PARSLEY, MINCED
>
> 3 CLOVES GARLIC, MINCED
>
> 15 BLACK OLIVES, PITTED OR WHOLE, WITH BRINE RINSED OFF††
>
> ½ FRESH LEMON

Wash, drain and coarsely chop chard into ½-inch pieces. Steam in a metal basket or colander placed over a pot of boiling water until chard wilts, about 2–3 minutes. Let sit in colander and press chard with the back of a large spoon to squeeze out excess water. Set aside. Cut preserved lemon into several pieces. Remove pulp and simmer rind in water for about 2 minutes to remove salt and bitter taste. Drain and chop rind into small pieces (yields about 2 teaspoons). Put chopped lemon rind, olive oil, paprika, cumin, pepper, cilantro, parsley, garlic and olives into a large pot. Cook about 2 minutes over medium heat, stirring constantly to make sure that the garlic and spices don't burn. Squeeze ½ fresh lemon into the pot. Stir and cook another 30 seconds. Add chard and continue to stir until all the liquid has evaporated.

*This recipe uses Swiss chard as a substitute for wild greens (*bakoola*). In Morocco this dish is commonly made with a wild, spinach-like plant (mallow) with large leaves.

†Available at stores carrying North African and Middle Eastern foods; also see *Resources,* p. 71, for mail-order sources of Moroccan foods. Preserved lemons are easy to make; see recipe, p. 68.

††Dry-cured black olives may be substituted.

Zahlouk

Cooked eggplant and tomato salad. Serves 6–10.

This recipe was provided by Halima Benayad, who is from the small town of Zawiya in north central Morocco near Meknès. She is a university student majoring in information sciences.

> 3 MEDIUM EGGPLANTS, ROASTED
>
> 3½ TABLESPOONS OLIVE OIL
>
> 3½ TABLESPOONS SALAD OIL
>
> 8 MEDIUM TO LARGE CLOVES GARLIC, CHOPPED
>
> 3 LARGE TOMATOES, PEELED AND CHOPPED INTO ½-INCH PIECES
>
> 1 CUP CILANTRO, CHOPPED

1 CUP FLAT-LEAF PARSLEY, CHOPPED

6 HEAPING TEASPOONS GROUND CUMIN

3 TEASPOONS PAPRIKA

¼ TEASPOON CAYENNE

3 TEASPOONS SALT, OR TO TASTE

Cut eggplants in half lengthwise and place face down on a cookie sheet. Place near flame in an oven with broiler set on high until eggplants are blackened and crisp, about 20–40 minutes. Remove and let cool, then scrape out the softened inside of the eggplant and as much of the inside of the skin as possible. The seeds, which are easy to take out at this point, can be removed if desired. Combine oils, garlic, tomatoes, cilantro, parsley and spices in a frying pan, fry a few minutes and then add eggplant. Cook, uncovered, over medium-low heat for 15–45 minutes, until all ingredients are soft. Correct spices if necessary. Serve salad in several small, shallow bowls if entrée is eaten from a communal dish, Moroccan style.

Matisha M'sla

Sweet plum tomato salad or jam. Makes about 2½ cups.

This recipe was provided by Paula Wolfert, who has lived in and traveled to many countries in the Mediterranean. Her many cookbooks about the cuisines of Morocco, southern France and the eastern Mediterranean are perennially popular. This cooked salad also is used as a preserve or is spread over certain stewed lamb dishes.

4 POUNDS PLUM TOMATOES, CORED AND SEEDED

2 TABLESPOONS EXTRA-VIRGIN OLIVE OIL

1½–2 TABLESPOONS HONEY

SCANT ½ TEASPOON CINNAMON

SALT AND FRESHLY GROUND PEPPER TO TASTE

1½ TEASPOONS ORANGE-FLOWER WATER*

1 TABLESPOON SESAME SEEDS, TOASTED

Preheat oven to 450°F. Arrange tomatoes on a large-rimmed baking sheet and bake for 1 hour, turning occasionally, until soft and blackened in spots. Cool, then peel and coarsely chop tomatoes.

Heat olive oil in a large frying pan until shimmering. Add tomatoes and cook over moderately high heat, stirring frequently, until all the liquid has evaporated and the tomatoes are sizzling and beginning to brown, about 8 minutes. Add honey and

[Matisha M'sla, *continued*]

cinnamon, season with salt and pepper and cook for 1 minute. Transfer salad to a bowl and refrigerate until cool, about 30 minutes. Stir in the orange-flower water and season again with salt and pepper, if desired. Sprinkle with sesame seeds.
*Available at stores carrying North African and Middle Eastern foods; also see *Resources,* p. 71, for mail-order sources of Moroccan foods.

Shlada Limun

Orange salad. Serves 4–8.

The recipe for this salad was provided by Susan Schaefer Davis, an anthropologist who has worked in Morocco off and on since her Peace Corps service there in 1965–67. She has written several articles and two books on Morocco: *Patience and Power: Women's Lives in a Moroccan Village,* and *Adolescence in a Moroccan Town.* Professor Davis is currently a consultant on international development.

> 4 NAVEL ORANGES, PREFERABLY SWEET
>
> GRANULATED SUGAR
>
> GROUND CINNAMON
>
> ORANGE-FLOWER WATER*
>
> WATER

Peel oranges, leaving them whole. Remove pith and slice them into ¼–½ inch slices. Overlap slices to form a circle on 2–3 salad or dessert plates to spread among guests, especially if everyone is eating from a central dish, Moroccan-style. Sprinkle slices with a little sugar, the amount depending on the sweetness of the oranges. Mix 1 teaspoon of orange-flower water with 2 teaspoons of water and drizzle the mixture over the slices with a spoon. Dust with cinnamon. This dish also can be served as a dessert.
*Available at stores carrying North African and Middle Eastern foods; also see *Resources,* p. 71, for mail-order suppliers of Moroccan food.

BREAD

Khobz Meqli

Semolina flatbread made in a skillet. Makes 12 5-inch loaves.

The recipe for this coarse flatbread was provided by Paula Wolfert, award-winning author of several classic cookbooks on the cuisines of the Mediterranean. The bread's grainy, dense texture makes it suitable to serve with greens (see recipe, p. 42) or tomato jam (see recipe, p. 45).

2¼ CUPS FINE SEMOLINA*

1 CUP COARSE SEMOLINA*

1 STICK PLUS 2 TABLESPOONS UNSALTED BUTTER, MELTED AND COOLED

1 TABLESPOON PLUS 1 TEASPOON SUGAR

½ TEASPOON SALT

1 CUP WARM WATER

Combine fine and coarse semolinas in a bowl. Add all but 2 tablespoons melted butter and rub mixture together with the hands until sandy. Stir in sugar and salt. Add ½ cup of the warm water and stir until crumbly. Let dough stand for 5 minutes. Stir remaining warm water into dough; it should be soft. Transfer to a food processor and pulse 30 times to combine. Turn dough out onto unfloured work surface. Using lightly buttered hands, knead it until silky, about 1–2 minutes. Cover dough loosely and let rest for 30 minutes.

Preheat a cast-iron grill pan or heavy frying pan over moderate heat. Cut dough into 12 equal pieces. On a lightly buttered work surface, press a piece of dough into a flat, 5-inch-round disk. Transfer the disk to a baking sheet, cover loosely with plastic and repeat to form the remaining flatbreads. Grill the breads over moderate heat, turning once, until blackened in spots and cooked through, about 4 minutes. Brush each flatbread with some of the remaining melted butter. Serve flatbreads hot off the grill, or wrap in foil and keep them warm in the oven (preheated to 250°F) for up to 30 minutes.

*Available at specialty food shops and stores carrying North African and Middle Eastern foods; also see *Resources,* p. 71, for mail-order sources of Moroccan foods. Do not use couscous semolina granules.

MAIN DISHES

Shaᶜriya Medfoun

Lamb stew buried in a nest of steamed vermicelli. Serves 4.

Futim-Zohra Oaehdghini (pictured on the front cover), chef de cuisine of the elegant Fint restaurant near the Kasbah Taourirt in Ouarzazate, provided this recipe.

1½ POUNDS LAMB, CUT INTO 1-INCH CUBES

1 SMALL RED ONION, CHOPPED

1 PACKET COLORANT (SAFFRON POWDER)*

1 PINCH REAL SAFFRON, CRUMBLED

1 TEASPOON SALT

1 TEASPOON PEPPER

[Sha^criya Medfoun, *continued*]

    1 TEASPOON GROUND GINGER

    ¾ CUP WATER

    2 TABLESPOONS OLIVE OIL

    3 CUPS FINE VERMICELLI, BROKEN INTO ½–1 inch pieces

    ¼ TEASPOON CINNAMON

    1 TABLESPOON POWDERED SUGAR

Put meat, onion, spices, water and one tablespoon oil in heavy saucepan. Simmer until meat is tender, about one hour, stirring occasionally. Add more water if necessary. Remove from heat and set aside in a warm place. Put water in the bottom of a two-piece *couscoussier* (steamer for steaming couscous) or in a large stockpot on which a colander fits snugly. Place the perforated top of the *couscoussier* on its bottom half (or the colander on the stockpot), making sure it does not touch the water. Seal both parts of the steamer by wrapping a strip of cheesecloth that has been wetted in a mixture of flour and water around the region where the two are joined. Overlap the fabric ends slightly and tuck them into the joint so the strip stays in place. A good seal is needed so steam from the boiling water escapes only through the holes in the top part of the *couscoussier* or colander. Place vermicelli in colander and steam, **uncovered**, until softened, about 10 minutes. Stir vermicelli occasionally. Remove top of *couscoussier* or colander from bottom pan and rinse vermicelli with hot water, then with cold water. Drain. Place vermicelli on platter and separate with fingers. Return vermicelli to top of *couscoussier* or colander, seal joint as before and steam again, **uncovered**, stirring occasionally until soft throughout. Repeat rinse steps. Put drained vermicelli on a platter and toss with remaining olive oil. Spread half the vermicelli in a 9-inch round baking dish. Mound the central area with the meat mixture, leaving the vermicelli at the edges uncovered. Completely cover meat and vermicelli with remaining vermicelli, so no meat is visible. Top with cinnamon and sugar mixture, and sprinkle with almonds. Place in 350°F oven for about 20 minutes or until heated throughout. Serve immediately in baking dish.

*A vivid orange powder, which includes ground turmeric and trace amounts of powdered saffron, is routinely added as a flavorant and colorant to many dishes. It is sold in small paper packets that are not readily available in the United States. A recommended substitute is ¼–½ teaspoon turmeric.

Tagine Kabab Maghdour bil Bid

Boulettes de "kefta" aux oeufs.

Meatballs in a tomato-based sauce with poached eggs. Serves 4.

The recipe for this popular dish was provided by Brahime Essadrati, chef de cuisine at the popular Palais Terrab restaurant in Meknès, which specializes in traditional and nouvelle Moroccan cuisine.

Meatballs

1 POUND GROUND LAMB

1 CLOVE GARLIC, MINCED

¼ CUP CILANTRO, CHOPPED

¼ CUP FLAT-LEAF PARSLEY, CHOPPED

Sauce

½ MEDIUM RED ONION, FINELY CHOPPED

8 SMALL TOMATOES, SEEDED AND FINELY CHOPPED

1 CLOVE GARLIC, MINCED

2 TABLESPOONS TOMATO PASTE

2 TEASPOONS PAPRIKA

2 TEASPOONS CUMIN

2 TEASPOONS SALT

2 TEASPOONS PEPPER

¼ TEASPOON CAYENNE

2 BAY LEAVES

1 BEEF BOUILLON CUBE

1 CUP WATER

¼ CUP CILANTRO, CHOPPED

¼ CUP FLAT-LEAF PARSLEY, CHOPPED

Poached eggs and garnish

4 EGGS

1 MEDIUM TOMATO, SLICED

PINCH CILANTRO, CHOPPED

PINCH FLAT-LEAF PARSLEY, CHOPPED

To make meatballs, mix together meat, garlic, cilantro and parsley. Form into ¾-inch meatballs and fry in a little oil in medium-size frying pan over high heat until browned. Remove from heat and set aside, covered. In a saucepan, combine sauce ingredients except cilantro and parsley, and simmer for 15 minutes over low heat. Remove bay leaves and strain sauce through a sieve. Place sauce and meatballs in *tagine* or heavy frying pan. Add cilantro and parsley, cover and cook 20 minutes over medium heat. Add water, if necessary, so the sauce is thin enough to poach eggs. Remove cover and break 4 eggs into the sauce. Cook until whites are set. To serve, garnish with tomato slices and a light sprinkle of chopped parsley and cilantro.

Lham bil Berquq wa Luz

Agneau ou boeuf aux pruneaux et aux amandes.

Lamb or beef with prunes and almonds. Serves 4–6.

This recipe was provided by Fatna Kotni, chef de cuisine at the Dar Marjana restaurant, which is housed in a beautiful converted palace in Marrakech. It is located just inside the medina (old city) near Bab Doukkala, one of the large gates in the medina walls.

>1 CUP PRUNES, PITTED
>
>1 TEASPOON GROUND GINGER
>
>2 STICKS CINNAMON
>
>1 PACKET COLORANT (SAFFRON POWDER)*
>
>2 TEASPOONS SALT
>
>1 TEASPOON PEPPER
>
>¼ CUP SUNFLOWER OIL
>
>3 POUNDS LAMB OR BEEF SHOULDER, CUT INTO 1½-INCH PIECES
>
>2 CUPS WATER
>
>2 LARGE RED ONIONS, FINELY SLICED
>
>¼ CUP SUGAR
>
>1 STICK CINNAMON
>
>1 TABLESPOON ORANGE-FLOWER WATER†
>
>½ CUP ALMONDS, BLANCHED AND TOASTED
>
>2 TABLESPOONS SESAME SEEDS, TOASTED

Cover prunes with water and set aside. In a *tagine* or large frying pan, mix ginger, cinnamon, colorant, salt, pepper and oil. Add meat and stir to coat well. Heat over low heat for about 5 minutes. Add water. Bring to a boil, reduce heat to low and simmer for about 1 hour, stirring occasionally. Add onions and simmer until meat is tender, about ½ hour more. Drain prunes and put them in a small saucepan. Add sugar, cinnamon and orange-flower water. Cook until prunes are plump and tender. Mound meat in the center of the *tagine* or heated serving platter and top with prunes. Garnish with almonds and sesame seeds.

*A vivid orange powder, which includes ground turmeric and trace amounts of powdered saffron, is routinely added as a flavorant and colorant to many dishes. It is sold in small paper packets that are not readily available in the United States. A recommended substitute is ¼–½ teaspoon turmeric and an optional pinch of saffron.

†Available at specialty food shops, and stores carrying North African and Middle Eastern foods; also see *Resources,* p. 71, for mail-order sources of Moroccan foods.

Seksu Beidaoui

Couscous à la viande et aux sept légumes.

Couscous with meat and seven vegetables. Serves 6.

Haja Rabha Bami and her daughter, Meriem Bami, provided the recipe for this classic dish. Both live in Marrakech. Rabha Bami makes couscous granules (actually a pasta) the traditional way. She rolls coarse and very fine particles of semolina moistened with water, using a circular motion of her fingers against the bottom of a round, flat dish (see photo, color insert). The granules she makes are so uniform in size that a sieve is not needed. Commercially available dried couscous granules, which will be used in this recipe, do not get as fluffy after steaming as artisanal ones.

Moroccan cooks typically prepare the stew and simultaneously steam and dry the couscous granules, using a two-part *couscoussier* or equivalent. The recipe has been simplified by the author to make it easier to coordinate the various steps in the preparation of both components of the dish. The first steaming and drying of the couscous is completed before the stew is started. The traditional procedure used by the Bamis, also described, can be followed if desired. See color insert for finished dish.

> ½ CUP DRIED CHICKPEAS (SOAKED IN WATER 24 HOURS)
>
> 2 CUPS DRIED COUSCOUS*
>
> WATER
>
> 2 POUNDS THICK LAMB SHOULDER CHOPS, CUT INTO 1½-INCH PIECES
>
> 5 TABLESPOONS VEGETABLE OIL
>
> 4 TOMATOES, CORED, SEEDED AND COARSELY CHOPPED
>
> 1 MEDIUM ONION, QUARTERED
>
> 1 TABLESPOON GROUND GINGER
>
> 1 TABLESPOON SALT
>
> 1 TABLESPOON PEPPER
>
> 1 PACKET COLORANT (SAFFRON POWDER)†
>
> 8 CUPS WATER
>
> 1 LARGE TURNIP, PEELED AND CUT INTO 1-INCH PIECES
>
> 1 LARGE CARROT, PEELED AND CUT INTO 1-INCH PIECES
>
> 1 MEDIUM ZUCCHINI SQUASH, QUARTERED AND CUT INTO 3-INCH PIECES
>
> 2 SMALL EGGPLANTS, HALVED
>
> 3 TABLESPOONS BUTTER

Drain chickpeas, discard hulls and put in a saucepan. Add cold water and cook, covered, on medium heat until tender, about 1 hour. Drain and set aside.

Put couscous in a bowl and cover with water. Stir briefly and drain through a sieve. Place washed couscous in a large baking tin with a rim at least 1 inch high. Spread

[Seksu Beidaoui, *continued*]

couscous evenly in the pan and set aside about 10 minutes. The granules will begin to swell. Lift and rake them with the fingers to work out any lumps that may have formed.

For the first steaming of couscous using the simplified recipe, put water in the bottom of a two-piece *couscoussier* or in a large stockpot on which a colander fits snugly. Place the perforated top of the *couscoussier* on its bottom half (or the colander on the stockpot), making sure it does not touch the water. Seal both parts of the steamer by wrapping a strip of cheesecloth that has been wetted in a mixture of flour and water around the region where the two are joined. Overlap the fabric ends slightly and tuck them into the joint so the strip stays in place. A good seal is needed so steam from the boiling water escapes only through the holes in the top part of the *couscoussier* or colander. If the colander has large holes, line it with a circle of cheesecloth. Bring the water to a boil. When steam rises up through the holes, carefully spoon the couscous from the baking pan into the top of the *couscoussier* or colander, reduce the heat to medium and steam, **uncovered**, for 20 minutes. Remove the couscous from the steamer and gently spread it out again in the large baking tin. Sprinkle 1 cup of lightly salted water over the couscous. Work granules with the fingers to remove any lumps that may have formed. Let dry for about 15 minutes and cover with a dampened cloth while preparing stew. Set top of *couscoussier* or colander aside.

Put meat, oil, tomatoes, onion, ginger, salt, pepper and colorant in the bottom of the *couscoussier* or stockpot, cover and cook over low heat for 15 minutes, stirring occasionally. Add water and chickpeas, cover and bring to a boil, then simmer for 1 hour. In the traditional method, the first steaming of the couscous occurs at this point, over steaming broth, prior to the addition of vegetables. Follow the same procedure for steaming couscous over water and drying it, as above. Cover with a dampened cloth and continue with recipe below.

Add turnips and carrots to stockpot, cover and simmer 25–30 minutes. Add zucchini and eggplant. Repace top of *couscoussier* on bottom (or colander on stockpot) and seal with cheesecloth strip as before. Work fingers through couscous in baking pan to break up any lumps, and spoon it into top part of *couscoussier* or colander and steam for the second time, **uncovered**, for 20 minutes. Occasionally lift granules of couscous with a fork to break up lumps that may have formed. The couscous steamed initially over water will acquire the delicious flavor of the stew during the second steaming.

To serve, transfer couscous to a large, heated serving platter. Add butter and mix with a fork to break up any lumps. Mound couscous and make a depression in the center of it. With a slotted spoon, put meat in depression and arrange vegetables around it radially. Spoon some broth over the couscous and serve additional broth in a bowl on the side.

*Couscous cooked in boiling water is not light and fluffy. Purchase regular couscous made of hard semolina flour, not instant. It is available at specialty food shops and

Middle Eastern markets; also see *Resources,* p. 71, for mail-order suppliers.

†A vivid orange powder, which includes ground turmeric and trace amounts of powdered saffron, is routinely added as a flavorant and colorant to many dishes. It is sold in small paper packets that are not readily available in the United States. A recommended substitute is $^1/_4$–$^1/_2$ teaspoon turmeric and an optional pinch of saffron.

Tagine Lham bil Khodra Fassi

Fès-style lamb stew with seasonal vegetables. Serves 4.

This recipe was provided by Zohra El Meterfi, chef de cuisine at the highly regarded Palais la Medina restaurant, located in the medina of Fès.

$^1/_2$ CUP CHICKPEAS (SOAKED IN WATER 24 HOURS)

1 MEDIUM CLOVE GARLIC, MINCED

1 TEASPOON GROUND GINGER

$^1/_2$ TEASPOON PEPPER

1 PACKET COLORANT (SAFFRON POWDER)*

2 TABLESPOONS OLIVE OIL

3 TABLESPOONS VEGETABLE OIL

$^1/_2$ CUP RED ONION, CHOPPED

2$^1/_4$ POUNDS LAMB SHOULDER OR SHANK, CUT INTO PIECES

1 CUP WATER

4 LARGE CARROTS, CUT INTO $^1/_2$-INCH PIECES

3 LARGE POTATOES, CUT INTO $^1/_2$-INCH PIECES

$^3/_4$ CUP CILANTRO, FINELY CHOPPED

$^1/_4$ CUP OLIVES PACKED IN OLIVE OIL†

1 PRESERVED LEMON, QUARTERED

Boil chickpeas until tender, about 1–1$^1/_2$ hours. Drain and set aside. In a large *tagine* (9- or 10-inch diameter base) or equivalent-size heavy frying pan, mix together garlic, ginger, pepper, colorant, olive oil, vegetable oil and onions to make marinade. Add meat and coat well with marinade. Cook mixture, uncovered, over high heat for 10 minutes, stirring frequently. Add water, cover and cook an additional 30 minutes over medium-high heat, stirring frequently. Add carrots and cook stew 10 minutes more. Then add remaining ingredients, including cooked chickpeas, and more water (about $^1/_2$ cup). Cook, covered, until potatoes are tender, basting occasionally with sauce. Mound stew into a cone shape and serve in the

[Tagine Lham bil Khodra Fassi, *continued*]
tagine. If the stew is cooked in a frying pan, serve it mounded into a cone shape on a heated platter.

*A vivid orange powder, which includes ground turmeric and trace amounts of powdered saffron, is routinely added as a flavorant and colorant to many dishes. It is sold in small paper packets that are not readily available in the United States. A recommended substitute is 1/4–1/2 teaspoon turmeric and an optional pinch of saffron.

†Available at specialty food shops and stores carrying North African and Middle Eastern foods; also see *Resources,* p. 71, for mail-order sources of Moroccan foods.

Lham bil Quq wa Gra^c Taxrifin

Agneau aux artichauts et aux courgettes.

Tagine of lamb with artichokes and zucchini. Serves 4.

The recipe for this tasty stew was provided by Nicole Rio, owner of the prominent Tobsil restaurant in Marrakech, which specializes in traditional and nouvelle Moroccan cuisine.

> 1/2 CUP OLIVE OIL
>
> 1 MEDIUM ONION, CHOPPED
>
> 1 CLOVE GARLIC, MINCED
>
> 1 TABLESPOON FLAT-LEAF PARSLEY, MINCED
>
> 1 TEASPOON WHITE PEPPER
>
> 2 TEASPOONS GROUND GINGER
>
> 2 TEASPOONS CUMIN
>
> 2 TEASPOONS SALT
>
> 1 PACKET COLORANT (SAFFRON POWDER)*
>
> 1 BAY LEAF
>
> 2 1/2 POUNDS LAMB SHOULDER (BONE-IN), CUT INTO 1 1/2-INCH PIECES
>
> 1 LARGE, RIPE TOMATO, CORED, SEEDED AND FINELY CHOPPED
>
> 1 CUP WATER
>
> 1 PRESERVED LEMON, QUARTERED†
>
> 3–4 MEDIUM ZUCCHINI SQUASH, UNPEELED
>
> 4 FRESH ARTICHOKES
>
> 1 TABLESPOON VINEGAR
>
> 2 CUPS WATER

Mix together olive oil, onion, garlic, parsley, white pepper, ginger, cumin, salt and colorant in *tagine* or large, heavy frying pan. Add bay leaf and meat. Cook meat, covered, over medium heat for 15–20 minutes until brown, stirring occasionally. Add tomato and water. Cover and simmer until meat is very tender, about 1 hour. Remove meat and keep warm in covered casserole in 200°F oven. Rinse preserved lemon quarters to remove salt and bitterness. Scoop out pulp and cut peel into small pieces. Add pulp and peel to sauce. Cut squash into 2-inch lengths and cut each piece in half. Add to sauce. Cut off artichoke stems and cut leaves about 1 inch from base. Remove and discard remaining part of leaves and "choke" (or "beard") above heart. Trim edges of artichoke hearts. As each is trimmed, place it in vinegar water to prevent discoloration. When all hearts are prepared, rinse them and add to sauce. Simmer vegetables until tender, about 20 minutes, stirring occasionally. Reheat meat on stove if necessary. Place vegetable mixture on top of meat and serve.

*A vivid orange powder, which includes ground turmeric and trace amounts of powdered saffron, is routinely added as a flavorant and colorant to many dishes. It is sold in small paper packets that are not readily available in the United States. A recommended substitute is ¹/₄–¹/₂ teaspoon turmeric and an optional pinch of saffron.

†Available at stores carrying North African and Middle Eastern foods; also see *Resources,* p. 71, for mail-order sources of Moroccan foods. Preserved lemons are easy to make; see recipe, p. 68.

Kabab

Brochettes.

Skewered meat. Serves 3–4.

This recipe was provided by Mohamed Kassi, chef de cuisine at the Hotel La Fibula de Dr^ca in Zagora, an oasis in the Dr^ca Valley in the south. The Moroccan version of this popular dish is made without the skewered vegetables.

> *Marinade*
>
> 1 TEASPOON CUMIN
>
> 1 PACKET COLORANT (SAFFRON POWDER)*
>
> 1 SMALL RED ONION, CHOPPED
>
> 1 SMALL TOMATO, CHOPPED
>
> ¼ CUP VEGETABLE OIL
>
> *Meat*
>
> 1 POUND LAMB, CUT INTO 1-INCH CUBES

[Kabab, *continued*]

Vegetables and spice coating

2 GREEN PEPPERS, CUT INTO 1½-INCH SQUARES

4 SMALL TOMATOES, QUARTERED

2 LARGE RED ONIONS, HALVED CROSSWAYS AND THEN QUARTERED

1 TEASPOON SALT

1 TEASPOON PEPPER

1 TEASPOON HOT PAPRIKA

4 PACKETS COLORANT (SAFFRON POWDER)*

1 TEASPOON CUMIN

Mix marinade ingredients together. Stir in meat and marinate for 24 hours in the refrigerator. Toss green pepper, tomatoes and onions with salt, pepper, paprika, colorant and cumin. Thread marinated meat and spice-coated vegetables on skewers and grill. For the Moroccan version, omit vegetables.

*A vivid orange powder, which includes ground turmeric and trace amounts of powdered saffron, is routinely added as a flavorant and colorant to many dishes. It is sold in small paper packets that are not readily available in the United States. A recommended substitute is ¼–½ teaspoon turmeric and an optional pinch of saffron.

Djaj M'qualli bil Hamd Marked wa Zitun I

Tajine de poulet au citron comfit.

Chicken with preserved lemons and olives. Serves 4.

Haja Fatema, chef de cuisine at the popular Palais Mnebhi restaurant in Fès, provided the recipe for this classic dish. A whole chicken is cooked in this version.

1 WHOLE CHICKEN, ABOUT 3½ POUNDS

SALT

2 TABLESPOONS SHALLOT, FINELY CHOPPED

½ CUP RED ONION, FINELY CHOPPED

1 TEASPOON GROUND GINGER

1 PACKET COLORANT (SAFFRON POWDER)*

2 TEASPOONS SALT

1 CUP WATER

6–8 SPRIGS CILANTRO, FOLDED INTO A BUNDLE AND TIED WITH STRING

¼ CUP VEGETABLE OIL

1 PRESERVED LEMON, QUARTERED†

¼ CUP VIOLET OLIVES††

¼ CUP OLIVE OIL

Rub chicken inside and out with salt. Rinse and pat dry. Mix shallot, onion, ginger, colorant and salt in a large bowl. Dredge chicken in marinade, using utensils to manipulate the chicken; the colorant stains and doesn't wash off immediately. Put chicken in *tagine* or large casserole. Add ½ cup of the water to the bowl containing the marinade. Stir to get all spices, onion and shallot off sides, and pour contents over chicken. Add cilantro, oil and remaining ½ cup of the water to *tagine* or casserole. Cover and cook over medium-low heat for about 1 hour, or until chicken is done and pulls easily off the bones. Occasionally turn chicken and baste with sauce. Briefly soak lemon in water to remove salt and bitterness. Cut pulp from rind. Mash and add to sauce. Cut rind into thin strips and add to sauce, along with olives and olive oil, and cook, covered, for another 10–15 minutes. Remove chicken to serving dish and keep warm. Cook sauce, uncovered, until reduced. Tilt *tagine* or casserole to remove excess oil with a spoon. Top chicken with reduced sauce and serve.

*A vivid orange powder, which includes ground turmeric and trace amounts of powdered saffron, is routinely added as a flavorant and colorant to many dishes. It is sold in small paper packets that are not readily available in the United States. A recommended substitute is ¼–½ teaspoon turmeric and an optional pinch of saffron.

†Available at stores carrying North African and Middle Eastern foods; also see *Resources,* p. 71, for mail-order sources of Moroccan foods. Preserved lemons are easy to make; see recipe, p. 68.

††Available at stores carrying North African and Middle Eastern foods; also see *Resources,* p. 71, for mail-order sources of Moroccan foods.

Djaj M'qualli bil Hamd Marked wa Zitun II

Tajine de poulet au citron comfit.

Chicken with preserved lemons and olives. Serves 4.

This recipe was provided by Jean-Marc Varin, executive chef of the esteemed El Mansour restaurant in the Hotel Meridien Tour Hassan in Rabat, the political capital of Morocco since 1912.

½ CUP RED ONION, CHOPPED

1 TABLESPOON GARLIC, FINELY CHOPPED

2 TEASPOONS GROUND GINGER

1 TEASPOON COARSE SALT

2 TEASPOONS GROUND WHITE PEPPER

10 THREADS SAFFRON, CRUSHED

[Djaj M'qualli bil Hamd Marked wa Zitun II, *continued*]

    1 PACKET COLORANT (SAFFRON POWDER)*

    3–4 POUNDS CHICKEN (THIGHS AND BREASTS)

    1 CUP WATER

    2 TABLESPOONS SUNFLOWER OIL

    8 SPRIGS CILANTRO, FOLDED INTO A BUNDLE AND TIED WITH STRING

    1 PRESERVED LEMON, QUARTERED†

    12 VIOLET OLIVES††

Mix onion, garlic, spices and colorant in a bowl. Dredge chicken pieces in mixture and place skin-side down in a *tagine* or casserole. Add water and oil to the bowl, stirring well to remove any spice mixture adhering to the sides. Pour liquid over chicken. Add cilantro. Cover and bring to a boil, then lower heat and simmer, covered, turning meat several times. When chicken is nearly cooked (about 45 minutes), add lemon quarters and olives and simmer, covered, another 10 minutes. Preheat oven to 200°F. Transfer meat from dish to a pan and keep warm in oven. Discard cilantro. Reduce sauce, uncovered. Tip pan and spoon off excess oil. Return meat to *tagine* or casserole, and spoon sauce, olives and lemon quarters over meat. Serve at once.

*A vivid orange powder, which includes ground turmeric and trace amounts of powdered saffron, is routinely added as a flavorant and colorant to many dishes. It is sold in small paper packets that are not readily available in the United States. A recommended substitute is $1/4$–$1/2$ teaspoon turmeric and an optional pinch of saffron.

†Available at stores carrying North African and Middle Eastern foods; also see *Resources,* p. 71, for mail-order sources of Moroccan foods. Preserved lemons are easy to make; see recipe, p. 68.

††Available at stores carrying North African and Middle Eastern foods; also see *Resources,* p. 71, for mail-order sources of Moroccan foods.

Djaj bil Tmer

Chicken stew with dates. Serves 4.

The recipe for this classic stew (*tagine*), which makes good use of one of Morocco's ubiquitous commodities—dates, was provided by Kitty Morse. Born and raised in Casablanca, she is author of many cookbooks about North African cuisine, including the popular *Cooking at the Kasbah: Recipes from My Moroccan Kitchen.*

    2 TABLESPOONS VEGETABLE OIL

    4 CHICKEN THIGHS

    4 CHICKEN LEGS

    ¼ CUP FLAT-LEAF PARSLEY, CHOPPED

2 TABLESPOONS CILANTRO, CHOPPED

1 GARLIC CLOVE, MINCED

½ TEASPOON GROUND CINNAMON

1 TEASPOON TURMERIC

1 TEASPOON GROUND GINGER

8 SAFFRON THREADS, TOASTED AND CRUSHED

1 CUP CHICKEN BROTH

½ CUP HONEY

½ POUND PITTED DATES

SALT AND FRESHLY GROUND BLACK PEPPER TO TASTE

In a Dutch oven, heat oil over medium heat and brown the chicken on all sides. Add parsley, cilantro, garlic, cinnamon, turmeric, ginger, saffron and broth. Cover, and cook until chicken is tender, 45–50 minutes. Preheat oven to 200°F. Transfer the chicken to a serving platter, and keep it warm in the oven. Bring the sauce in the pan to a simmer. Add honey and stir until the sauce thickens somewhat. Add dates, mashing them down slightly with a fork, and cook for 8–10 minutes. Season with salt and pepper. Return the chicken to the sauce, and heat through. To serve, mound the chicken on the serving platter. Spoon the sauce and dates over the top. Serve with plenty of crusty bread or couscous to mop up the sauce.

Djaj bil ᶜAssal wa Romman wa Luz

Cornish hen with honey, pomegranate juice and toasted almonds. Serves 8–10.

Rafih and Rita Benjelloun, owners of the Imperial Fez restaurant in Atlanta, Georgia, provided the recipe for this dish. It is one of several elegant dishes that chef Rafih prepared at the prestigious James Beard House in New York City to showcase Moroccan food.

¼ CUP OLIVE OIL

5 16-OUNCE CORNISH HENS, QUARTERED

2 LARGE ONIONS, FINELY CHOPPED

3 CUPS WATER

½ CUP FLAT-LEAF PARSLEY, FINELY CHOPPED

2 TABLESPOONS GROUND GINGER

1 TEASPOON CINNAMON

½ TEASPOON NUTMEG

PINCH GROUND CLOVES

[Djaj bil ᶜAssal wa Romman wa Luz, *continued*]

    GENEROUS PINCH OF SAFFRON

    SALT TO TASTE

    1 TEASPOON PEPPER

    ½ CUP POMEGRANATE JUICE*

    ½ CUP HONEY

    1 CUP RAISINS

      Garnish

    1 CUP BLANCHED ALMONDS, ROASTED

    ¼ CUP SESAME SEEDS, TOASTED

Heat olive oil in a large casserole or frying pan. Sauté Cornish hens and onions over medium-high heat until hens are browned, stirring occasionally. Add water, parsley, ginger, cinnamon, nutmeg, clove, saffron, salt and pepper. Cover and cook over medium-low heat for about 35 minutes or until done, turning once. Transfer hens to a large serving platter and keep warm. Add pomegranate juice, honey and raisins to remaining sauce. Simmer for 3–5 minutes. Pour sauce over hens. Garnish with almonds and sesame seeds.

*Pomegranate syrup or molasses can be substituted for pomegranate juice. Use 1½ teaspoons diluted in ½ cup water. Available at specialty food shops and stores carrying North African and Middle Eastern foods; also see *Resources,* p. 71, for mail-order sources of Moroccan foods.

Tagine bil Hut

Tajine de poisson à la Marocaine.

Fish cooked in the classic "dry" chermula *marinade*. Serves 3–4.

This recipe was provided by Kamel Hassan, sous chef at the El Korsan restaurant at the El Minzah hotel in Tangier.

    2 TABLESPOONS PAPRIKA

    1 TABLESPOON CUMIN

    2 TEASPOONS SALT

    2 TABLESPOONS CILANTRO, FINELY CHOPPED

    2 CLOVES GARLIC, FINELY CHOPPED

    ½ CUP OLIVE OIL

    ¼ CUP WHITE VINEGAR

    1½ POUNDS FISH FILLETS*

2 MEDIUM GREEN BELL PEPPERS, CUT INTO ½-INCH STRIPS

2 LARGE RIPE TOMATOES, CUT INTO ½-INCH SLICES

1 CUP WATER

2 SMALL, WHOLE HOT RED PEPPERS

Mix together paprika, cumin, salt, cilantro, garlic, olive oil and vinegar. Put half of the marinade in a ceramic dish and coat fillets well. Marinate for one hour, turning occasionally. Place pepper strips in a single layer on the bottom of a heavy ovenproof frying pan. Put the fish on the bed of green peppers and cover with unused marinade, uniformly covering fish. Top with tomato slices. Add water and hot peppers. Bring to a boil, uncovered, over a hot flame. Then transfer the pan to the top shelf of an oven heated on the broiler setting to 400°F. Cook for 10–15 minutes until fish is done and tomatoes are nicely seared. To serve, transfer fish to heated *tagine* or serving dish.

*Use white-fleshed fish such as halibut, sea bream, haddock or cod.

Bousaif bil Chermula

Braised swordfish seasoned with a "dry" marinade. Serves 4.

Mustapha Haddouch provided the recipe for this delicious fish dish, a family favorite that was prepared when he was growing up in Tangier, a city on the northern coast of Morocco. Mustapha owns Haddouch Gourmet Imports, based in Seattle, Washington, and his high-quality Moroccan food products are esteemed by professional chefs and weekend gourmets.

2 MEDIUM POTATOES, CUT INTO THIN SLICES

1 MEDIUM RED ONION, CUT INTO THIN SLICES

1 LARGE CARROT, CUT INTO THIN STRIPS ABOUT 2 INCHES LONG

2 TOMATOES, CUT INTO THIN SLICES

SALT AND PEPPER TO TASTE

4 SWORDFISH STEAKS, ¾ TO 1-INCH THICK

1½ CUPS WATER

¼ CUP WHITE VINEGAR

1 TABLESPOON KOSHER SALT

Marinade

3 CLOVES GARLIC, MINCED

½ CUP FLAT-LEAF PARSLEY, MINCED

½ CUP CILANTRO, MINCED

[Bousaif bil Chermula, *continued*]

    1½ TABLESPOONS PAPRIKA

    1 TEASPOON CUMIN

    ¼ TEASPOON CHILE PASTE

    ¼ TEASPOON BLACK PEPPER

    JUICE OF 1 LEMON

    2 TABLESPOONS OLIVE OIL

      Topping

    1 GREEN BELL PEPPER

    1 LEMON, SLICED

    SALT AND PEPPER TO TASTE

Layer a 9- to 10-inch *tagine* or ceramic baking dish with slices of potatoes, onions, carrots and one of the tomatoes to prevent the fish from sticking to it. Add salt and pepper to taste. Set aside. Soak the swordfish steaks (and bones) in water, vinegar and salt for 10 minutes. In a flat dish, mix together marinade: garlic, parsley, cilantro, paprika, cumin, chile paste, pepper, lemon juice and olive oil. Rinse steaks with water, coat each side well with marinade and place in a single layer on top of the vegetable slices in the *tagine*. Top the fish with slices of green pepper, lemon and remaining tomato, and sprinkle with salt and pepper to taste. Add a little water (about ⅛ cup) to the marinade remaining in the dish to loosen it, and pour over the fish. Bring to a boil on the stovetop. Lower heat and simmer, covered, for about 30 minutes, or until the fish is done.

DESSERTS

Briwat bil Luz

"Briouates" aux Amandes.

Honey-soaked, triangle-shaped pastries filled with almond paste. Makes about 2½ dozen.

This recipe was provided by Elkifly Najah. She is the chef de cuisine at L'Institut de Technologie Hotelière et Touristique de Fès, a government-sponsored school teaching the art of Moroccan gastronomy and hotel management. In Morocco these pastries are made with *warka,* an ultrathin, almost transparent sheet of cooked pastry made of small, overlapping circles of dough (see *Foods & Flavors Guide*). Ready-made sheets of phyllo dough will be substituted for *warka.*

    1 POUND WHOLE ALMONDS, BLANCHED

    1 CUP SUGAR

2 TEASPOON BUTTER

½ TEASPOON CINNAMON

1 PACKAGE PHYLLO DOUGH*

MELTED BUTTER FOR PASTRY

1 EGG YOLK

VEGETABLE OIL FOR FRYING

1–2 CUPS HONEY

Toast half the nuts in the oven for 15–20 minutes at 300°F. Cool. Grind all nuts finely in a food processor. Add sugar, butter and cinnamon and grind to a paste. Remove from processor and knead into a ball. Add more butter if the paste is too crumbly. Form into 1-inch balls, flatten a bit and set aside.

To prepare pastry, spread open the sheets of dough and with sharp scissors cut 19 sheets in half the short way. Half sheets will be about 9 inches wide and 14 inches long. Remove one half sheet from the stack and place it on a clean work surface. To keep the remaining sheets from drying out, cover with plastic wrap topped with a slightly damp towel. With the short end of the pastry sheet facing you, brush the surface with melted butter. Fold in thirds, lengthwise, by folding one side over the middle, then the other, to form a strip about 3 inches wide. Place a flattened ball of almond paste on the buttered sheet close to the end nearest you. Bring one corner of the dough up and over the ball to make a triangle. Make the next fold by bending the triangular-shaped covered ball away from you. Continue folding away from you, adding thicknesses to the triangular-shaped pastry, until you reach the end of the strip. Put a little egg yolk on the end of the strip and tuck it into a fold to seal.

In a heavy pot, fry pastry triangles in moderately hot oil until golden, turning over once during frying. Drain with a slotted spoon and transfer the pastry into a saucepan of simmering honey. Leave for a few minutes, turning once, to let the pastry absorb the honey. Drain with a slotted spoon and remove to a plate to cool.

*Follow thawing instructions on package, so sheets are ready to use when needed.

Sfinge bil Tut Rumi

Deep-fried strawberry fritters. Makes 2 dozen.

This recipe was provided by Abdul Bensaid and Cindy Brown, owners of Nadia's, a restaurant in Madison, Wisconsin, featuring Moroccan and southern Mediterranean cuisine. Bensaid was a chef in Morocco and several European countries before moving to the United States. These fritters are a modification of the popular Moroccan doughnut eaten in the morning with mint tea (see illustration, p. 30).

24 STRAWBERRIES

3 EGGS

[Sfinge bil Tut Rumi, *continued*]

½ CUP SUGAR

½ TEASPOON VANILLA

1 CUP FLOUR

OIL FOR DEEP-FRYING

Wash strawberries and discard leaves and stem. Pat dry with a paper towel and set aside. Beat eggs well. Blend in sugar and vanilla. When well mixed, slowly add flour and beat batter until smooth. Heat oil in heavy saucepan to 370°F. Working with a few at a time, put strawberries in batter and roll around to cover completely. Drop into the hot oil, turning several times. Remove when golden brown, about 1–2 minutes, and drain on absorbent paper. Sprinkle with confectioner's sugar, cinnamon sugar or honey. They are best when served warm.

Ka^cb el Ghzal

Cornes de gazelle.

Gazelle's horns. Makes 2½ dozen.

The recipe for these delicate crescent-shaped pastries filled with almond paste was provided by Elkifly Najah. She is the chef de cuisine at L'Institut de Technologie Hotelière et Touristique de Fès, a government-sponsored school teaching the art of Moroccan gastronomy and hotel management.

Almond paste

1¾ CUP WHOLE ALMONDS, BLANCHED

4–5 TABLESPOONS MELTED BUTTER, COOLED

¾–1 CUP CASTOR SUGAR (OR 1 CUP POWDERED SUGAR)

¼ TEASPOON ALMOND EXTRACT

Dough

2 CUPS FLOUR

¼ TEASPOON SALT

1 TEASPOON BUTTER

1 EGG

½ CUP ORANGE-FLOWER WATER*

Grind nuts finely in a food processor. Add butter, sugar and almond extract and grind to a paste. Remove from processor and knead to form a ball. Wrap in plastic and chill.

To make dough, blend flour with salt and cut butter into the mixture. Add egg and mix well. Slowly stir in orange-flower water. Gently knead dough until uniformly blended. Cover with plastic wrap and let rest 30 minutes at room temperature.

To make filling, take about 2 teaspoons almond paste and roll into a sausage shape that is wider at the middle and about 2 inches long. If the paste is crumbly, squeeze with the hands to warm it slightly and make it more compact. Shape the remaining almond paste in a similar manner, making a total of about 32 pieces. Cover and set aside.

To roll the dough, rub a little vegetable oil over the work surface and rolling pin. Take about ¼ of the dough, form a ball and roll it out away from you into a long rectangle about 3–4 inches wide and about ¹⁄₁₆ inch thick. With the short end of the rectangle facing you, place one rolled piece of filling the long way near the edge of the dough. Gently tug the dough just this side of the filling to stretch it thinner, being careful not to let it tear. Wrap the stretched dough up and over the filling, letting its edge touch the dough on the other side of the filling. Press the two thicknesses of dough together close to the filling, using the thumb to make a good seal. Cut the pastry out with a pastry wheel, making the cut ⅛ to ¼ inch away from the pastry. With thumb and forefinger of both hands, hold the pastry on each side and bend it into a slight crescent shape. Slowly lift pastry off working surface and place on a lightly oiled baking pan. Prick the pastries in a couple of places so they don't puff up during baking. Continue forming seven more pastries with the rest of the rolled dough. Divide the remaining dough into 3 parts and follow the same procedures. Bake for 15 minutes at 325°F. Pastries should remain pale when baked.

Remove from pan and leave plain or brush lightly with orange-flower water and roll in confectioners' sugar while still warm.

*Available at stores carrying North African and Middle Eastern foods; also see *Resources,* p. 71, for mail-order suppliers of Moroccan food.

Feqqas

Biscotti-like, twice-baked cookie rounds. Makes 10–12 dozen.

Abdul Bensaid and Cindy Brown, owners of of Nadia's, a restaurant in Madison, Wisconsin, featuring Moroccan and southern Mediterranean cuisine, provided the recipe for these crunchy, tasty cookies. They traditionally are dunked in mint tea.

> 2 PACKETS ACTIVE DRY YEAST
>
> ½ CUP LUKEWARM WATER (100–110°F)
>
> 3¾ CUPS FLOUR
>
> ¼ TEASPOON SALT

[Feqqas, *continued*]

> ⅞ CUP SUGAR
>
> ½ TABLESPOON ANISEEDS*
>
> ½ TABLESPOON TOASTED SESAME SEEDS
>
> ¼ CUP RAISINS (OPTIONAL)
>
> ¼ CUP ALMONDS, COARSELY CHOPPED (OPTIONAL)
>
> ½ CUP MELTED BUTTER, COOLED
>
> 5 TABLESPOONS ORANGE-FLOWER WATER†
>
> 1–2 TABLESPOONS LUKEWARM WATER

Mix yeast in ½ cup lukewarm water and let sit in a warm place for about 2 hours. Put flour, salt, sugar, and seeds (and raisins and nuts, if desired) in a large bowl and mix well. Stir in yeast mixture and butter and blend well. Add orange-flower water and 1–2 tablespoons lukewarm water and mix well. Add a little more lukewarm water if necessary. Dough will be firm. Knead for several minutes until smooth and then divide dough into 4 pieces.

Shape into balls and place on a lightly floured board. Let rise in a warm place, covered, for 2 hours. Roll balls into 12-inch cylinders of uniform thickness. Place on cookie trays, 2 rolls to a 10″ × 15″ tray, covered, and let rise in a warm place until doubled, about 2 hours. The rolls will flatten somewhat. Prick rolls in several places with a fork. Bake in oven preheated to 350°F for 20 minutes, or until just turning a golden color. The rolls will not be baked completely. Let sit overnight, uncovered, on a rack. The next day, cut rolls into ¼-inch slices. Lay slices flat on ungreased baking trays and bake for 8–10 minutes at 350°F until browned and dry. Cool and store covered to keep cookies crispy.

*If almonds and raisins are added to the dough, aniseeds may be omitted, if desired.
†Available at stores carrying North African and Middle Eastern foods; also see *Resources,* p. 71, for mail-order sources of Moroccan foods.

Ghoriba

Semolina cookies. Makes 3 dozen.

Abdul Bensaid and Cindy Brown, owners of Nadia's, a restaurant in Madison, Wisconsin, featuring Moroccan and southern Mediterranean cuisine, provided the recipe for these popular cookies. Chef Bensaid is from the fishing port of Asilah on the Atlantic coast, south of Tangier.

> ⅛ CUP BUTTER
>
> ⅛ CUP PEANUT OIL
>
> 3 EGGS

2½ CUPS POWDERED SUGAR

3 CUPS FINE SEMOLINA (NOT COUSCOUS GRANULES)

1 TEASPOON BAKING POWDER

¾ TEASPOON VANILLA

⅛ TEASPOON SALT

ORANGE-FLOWER WATER*

POWDERED SUGAR FOR ROLLING

Preheat oven to 350°F. Melt butter, mix with peanut oil and set aside. In a large bowl beat eggs with sugar until fluffy. Add butter and oil mixture, and blend well. Mix together semolina, baking powder, vanilla and salt, and add to bowl. Stir well. Before shaping each cookie, dip your fingers into some orange-flower water to help prevent the dough from sticking to your hands. Take heaping tablespoonfuls of dough and roll each into a ball. The fragrant water will be absorbed by the dough and make them even tastier. Gently press balls into some powdered sugar, generously coating them on one side. Put slightly flattened cookies on a buttered baking sheet, sugar side up, leaving about two inches between cookies. Bake 15–20 minutes. Cookies will remain the color of the dough.

*Available at stores carrying North African and Middle Eastern foods; also see *Resources,* p. 71, for mail-order suppliers of Moroccan food.

MISCELLANEOUS

Amlou

Argan *almond spread*. Serves many.

This recipe was contributed by Hicham and Kimberly Ouhirra, co-founders of Exotica Oils, Inc., sole supplier of US certified toasted or natural organic *argan* oil from Morocco. Hicham Ouhirra comes from the village of Oulmes in the Middle Atlas Mountains.

6 OUNCES ALMONDS, SALTED AND ROASTED

7 TABLESPOONS TOASTED *ARGAN* OIL*

3 TABLESPOONS HONEY

Grind almonds in food processor to desired texture. Stir in *argan* oil tablespoon at a time. Blend until smooth. Stir in honey, manually a time. Mix well. Store at room temperature. Serve on bread.

*See *Resources,* p. 71, for mail-order source of *argan* oil.

Hamd Marked

Preserved lemons.

> 6 LEMONS
>
> ¼ CUP SALT
>
> FRESHLY SQUEEZED LEMON JUICE

Cut lemons into quarters, leaving about the last inch at the bottom uncut. Spread the quarters apart and cover pulp with salt. Bring quarters back together and place lemon in a clean glass jar. Repeat with the remaining lemons. With a wooden spoon, press down on the lemons to release some juice. Lemons can be cut in half if it is easier to pack the jar. Add remaining salt and enough freshly squeezed juice to cover the lemons completely, leaving some air space in the jar. Cap jar and gently shake to distribute added salt and juice. Leave jar at room temperature for one month, shaking once daily to distribute salt and juice. Use a wooden spoon or skewer to remove lemons as needed. Wash with water to remove salt and bitterness before use. Both pulp and peel can be used. Refrigerate lemons after opening jar. They will keep for about 6 months in the refrigerator.

Shopping in Morocco's Food Markets

Helpful Tips

The *Souks*

Learning more about Moroccan food in the outdoor *souks* is an adventure. Be prepared to ask, "What is this called?" because foods aren't labeled (see *Helpful Phrases,* p. 75). If you intend to buy, it is expected that you haggle over the price. Goods will be cheapest in the *souks*. Interestingly, women shoppers (but not vendors) are scarce because the rural marketplaces in particular are a man's domain. It is amusing to see men shopping for the groceries, knowing how they avoid the kitchen!

The markets farthest afield from the tourist path will take you to another world. A favorite is the Wednesday *souk* between Tangier and Chaouen, Souk el Arba des Beni Hassan. The more unusual items will be found in the spice and herb stalls. No matter what container they are in, the ingredients will be heaped in towering mounds, and the palette of colors will be pleasing. One of the more exotic items to be found is called *tamarrat,* meaning "beard of an old man." It is an aromatic, gray-green lichen sold in the south. Today it primarily is used in perfumery, but in southern Morocco it can be a flavorant for tea, stews and couscous dishes, too. Saffron is very popular and expensive. Beware that some vendors package safflower with some threads of saffron in it. The mixture may smell like saffron, but isn't. Small packets of "poor man's" saffron—mostly turmeric with a bit of saffron—are sold in boxes of 25 or so, which are scattered among the mounded spices. The label on the box says "Colorant Alimentaire Synthetique."

So many images in the markets beg for photographic capture. Moroccans, however, are reticent about having their picture taken. Always ask first.

The Indoor Markets

Food shopping indoors ranges from neighborhood convenience shops (*hanut* and the larger *epicerie*) to sizable French-style supermarkets (*supermarché*) in the larger cities, which are located either centrally in the new part of town or in the outskirts. These markets are one of many French influences that derive from the French occupancy of Morocco in the early 20th century. Markets carry a wide assortment of edible and nonedible items. You may be tempted to get the makings for a tasty picnic. For convenience, remember to pack some lightweight tableware and a pocket knife before leaving home!

The following abbreviated list of weights in transliterated Moroccan Arabic proved sufficient to get the quantities we wanted. Corresponding approximate weights in pounds are included.

> *tmen kilu:* eighth kilo, or ¼ pound
> *rub^c kilu:* quarter kilo, or ½ pound
> *nuss kilu:* half kilo, or 1 pound

If you are considering bringing food back to the United States, check with the US Customs Service beforehand to see which items or categories of items are allowed. Ask for the latest edition of publication number 512. Changes in regulations that occurred after publication can be obtained by writing to:

Assistant Commissioner
Office of Inspection and Control
US Customs Service
Washington, DC 20229

A Health Precaution

Wherever you travel, choose your food vendors with care, following the same criteria used at home. Don't ask for trouble. Some serious diseases can be transmitted by eating unclean produce. Make sure the produce looks fresh and clean. Should there be any doubt, look for stalls that appear popular with the local people. Bottled water is readily available and is a wise choice.

Resources

Mail-Order Suppliers of Moroccan Food Items

Morrocan ingredients can be found in stores specializing in North African or Middle Eastern foods and in many supermarkets. Natural food stores are also a good source of items such as couscous, which often is stocked in help-yourself bins. Please do not be tempted to buy packages of instant couscous. The grains aren't nearly as fluffy and tasty when boiled. Refer to the recipe for preparing couscous on p. 51. The extra effort pays off in the eating! We also encourage you to try cooking with *argan* oil; some of the most celebrated chefs around the world are discovering the exotic oil that the Berbers have enjoyed for centuries in Morocco.

Several mail-order suppliers of Moroccan food items are listed below. Some have a catalog or brochure of their products, and all have websites. We would appreciate knowing if a listed store no longer handles mail orders. Please also bring to our attention mail-order suppliers of Moroccan ingredients not included here.

At the end of each store's entry, we list the item(s) they supply for recipes in this guidebook.

Haddouch Gourmet Imports
1445 Elliot Ave. W
Seattle, WA 98119
Tel: 866-445-5566
Tel: 206-382-1706
Fax: 206-382-1958
www.haddouch.com
info@haddouch.com
(preserved lemons; olive oil; olives)

Sultan's Delight
PO Box 090302
Brooklyn, NY 11209
Tel: 800-852-5046
Fax: 718-745-2563
www.sultansdelight.com
sultansdelight@aol.com
catalog (orange-flower water; rosewater)

Ameerah Imports
2285 Peachtree Rd., Suite 100
Atlanta, GA 30309
Tel: 404-351-0430
Fax: 404-351-1272
www.ameerahimports.com
ghita@imperialfez.com
(cookware: *couscoussier,*
tagine; spices)

Exotica Oils, Inc.
838 Eastlake Club Dr.
Oldsmar, FL 34677
Tel: 727-786-6213
Fax: 727-786-7103
www.exoticaoils.com
info@exoticaoils.com
(cold-pressed, toasted or virgin
argan oil)

Oasis Date Gardens
PO Box 757
Thermal, CA 92274
Tel: 800-827-8017
Fax: 760-399-1068
www.oasisdategardens.com
catalog
(dates, dried fruit, nuts)

Volubilis Imports, Inc.
9380 Activity Rd., Suite J
San Diego, CA 92126
Tel: 858-530-0303
Fax: 858-530-8010
sales@volubilis2000.com
www.volubilis2000.com
(Moroccan wine and beer)

Travel Agencies

Two travel agencies, Travel in Style and Unitours, have teamed up to offer an exciting trip called the "Culinary Tour to Morocco." Joan Peterson, author of this guidebook, leads the tour. For more information or to request a flyer, please visit the author's website (www.ginkgopress.com) or contact the agencies, below. Join Joan in getting to the heart of the culture through an exploration of Morocco's delicious cuisine!

Travel in Style
1255 Post St., Suite 506
San Francisco, CA 94109
Tel: 415-440-1124
Tel: 888-466-8242
Fax: 603-297-3207
travelinstyle.com
info@travelinstyle.com

Unitours
127, Bd Mohamed V, Guéliz
Marrakech, Morocco
Tel: 212 44 44 69 13
Fax: 212 44 44 69 14
pbami@unitoursmaroc.ma
www.unitoursmaroc.ma

Another culinary tour is led by Kitty Morse, author of several Moroccan cookbooks. The tour includes cooking demonstrations in her family home, a restored pasha's residence south of Casablanca. For information, contact Natalie Tuomi at:

Carefree Vacations
2727 Roosevelt St., Suite B
Carlsbad, California 92008
Tel: 800-533-2779
Tel: 760-720-3454
Fax: 760-729-2482
ntuomi@sdtg.com

Some Useful Organizations to Know About

Moroccan National Tourism Offices

The addresses listed below are for the Moroccan Tourism Offices in the United States. Their staffs can assist you with your travel planning.

20 East 46th St., Suite 1201
New York, NY 10017
Tel: 212-557-2520
Fax: 212-949-8148

PO Box 22663
Lake Buena Vista, FL 32830
Tel: 407-827-5337
Fax: 407-827-0146

International Organizations

We are members of two international organizations that promote good will and understanding between people of different cultures. These organizations, Servas and The Friendship Force, share similar ideals but operate somewhat differently.

Servas

Servas, from the Esperanto word meaning "serve," is a non-profit system of travelers and hosts. Servas members travel independently and make their own contacts with fellow members in other countries, choosing hosts with attributes of interest from membership rosters. It is a wonderful way to get to know people, be invited into their homes as a family member, share experiences and help promote world peace.

For more information about membership in Servas, write or call:

US Servas Committee, Inc.
11 John St., Room 505
New York, NY 10038
Tel: 212-267-0252
Fax: 212-267-0292
www.usservas.org
info@servas.org

The Friendship Force

The Friendship Force is a non-profit organization, which also fosters good will through encounters between people of different backgrounds. Unlike Servas, Friendship Force members travel in groups to host countries. Both itinerary and travel arrangements are made by a member acting as exchange director. These trips combine stays with a host family and group travel within the host country.

For more information on membership in The Friendship Force, write:

The Friendship Force
34 Peachtree St., Suite 900
Atlanta, GA 30303
Tel: 404-522-9490
ffi@friendship-force.org
http://www.friendshipforce.org

Helpful Phrases

For Use in Restaurants and Food Markets

In the Restaurant

These transliterated Moroccan Arabic phrases will help you order food, learn about dishes you order, and determine what regional specialties are available. To help pronounce each transliteration, a phonetic interpretation is written below it. Syllables in capital letters are accented. To simplify pronouncing an *l* at the beginning of a word when followed by a consonant, the *l* sound was transferred to the ending of the previous word. Superscripted c (c) is a gutteral sound, far back in the mouth, as in "baa" of a sheep; *gh* is a gargling noise with a slight *r* sound; *kh* resembles a spitting sound.

DO YOU HAVE A MENU?	Wash kayn menoo?
	Wahsh cane MEN-oo?
MAY I SEE THE MENU?	Wash yumkin nshuuf l-menoo?
	Wahsh YOOM-kin n-SHOO-ful MEN-oo?
WHAT DO YOU RECOMMEND? (WHAT'S GOOD?)	Shnu mizyan?
	Shnoo mee-zee-ANNE?
DO YOU HAVE . . . HERE? (ADD AN ITEM FROM THE MENU GUIDE OR THE FOODS & FLAVORS GUIDE.)	Wash cindkum . . . hnayya?
	Wahsh END-koom . . . heh-NIGH-yah?

Helpful Phrases

WHAT IS THE "SPECIAL" FOR
TODAY?
(WHAT'S GOOD TODAY?)

Shnu mizyan annaharda?
Shnoo mee-zee-ANNE en-nah-HAR-dah?

DO YOU HAVE ANY SPECIAL
REGIONAL DISHES?

Wash ᶜindkum shay makla
mhalliyya?
*Wahsh END-koom sheh MEHK-lah
meh-hell-LEE-yah?*

IS THIS DISH SPICY/HOT?

Wash hadi l-makla harra?
Wahsh HAD-eel MEHK-lah HAHR-rah?

WE WOULD LIKE (TO
ORDER) . . .

Allah ykhaleek, kanbghiyu
(natlub) . . .
*Ahl-LAH ee-hall-LEEK can-BREE-yoo
(NAHT-lube) . . .*

WHAT ARE THE INGREDIENTS IN
THIS DISH?
(WHAT IS IN THIS DISH?)

Shnu kayn fee hadi l-makla?
Shnoo cane fee HAD-eel MEHK-lah?

WHAT ARE THE SEASONINGS IN
THIS DISH?

Shnu al ᶜatriyaat fi hadi l-makla?
*Shnoo el ah-tree-YAT fee HAD-eel
MEHK-lah?*

THANK YOU VERY MUCH. THE
FOOD IS (VERY) DELICIOUS.

Barak Allahu feek. Hadi l-makla
ldeeda bizaaf.
*Bah-rahk Ahl-LAH-who feek. HAD-
eel MEHK-lah lah-DEE-dah bee-ZAF.*

In the Market

The following phrases will help you make purchases and learn more about unfamiliar produce, spices and herbs.

WHAT ARE THE REGIONAL
FRUITS AND VEGETABLES?

Shnu alfawaakee wa lkhudar mhalliyya?
Shnoo el-fah-WACK-ee wahl HOOD-ar meh-hell-LEE-yah?

WHAT IS THIS CALLED?

Shnu smeet hada?
Shnoo smeet HAD-ah?

DO YOU HAVE . . . HERE?
(ADD AN ITEM FROM THE
FOODS & FLAVORS GUIDE.)

Wash ᶜindkum . . . hnayya?
Wahsh END-koom . . . heh-NIGH-yah?

MAY I TASTE THIS?

Wash yumkin nduqq hada?
Wahsh YOOM-kin en-DUHK HAD-ah?

WHERE CAN I BUY
FRESH . . . ?

Feen nshteree . . . triyya?
Feen nsh-TAIR-ree . . . TREE-yah?

HOW MUCH IS THIS PER
KILOGRAM (KG)?

Bi shhaal hada l'kilu?
Bish-HAL HAD-ahl KEE-loo?

I WOULD LIKE TO BUY ½ KILO-
GRAM (KG) OF THIS/THAT.

Kanbghee nshteri nuss kilu dyal hada.
Can-BREE nsh-TAIR-ree nuss KEE-loo dee-YAHL HAD-ah.

MAY I PHOTOGRAPH THIS?

Wash yumkin nkhud tsweera?
Wahsh YOOM-kin n-HOOD TSWEE-rah?

Other Useful Phrases

It helps to see a transliterated Moroccan Arabic word or phrase in writing, because certain letters in this language have distinctly different sounds than in English. Moroccan Arabic has more letters than the Roman alphabet; there are 31 consonants and 6 vowels. The following phrase is handy if you want to see what you are hearing.

PLEASE WRITE THAT ON MY PIECE OF PAPER.

Uktub hada fee l'warqa, allah ykhalleek.

Ook-TOOB HAD-ah feel WAR-kah ahl-LAH ee-hal-LEEK.

Interested in bringing home books about Moroccan food?

WHERE CAN I BUY A MOROCCAN COOKBOOK IN ENGLISH?

Feen nshteree kitaab tabkh maghrabi bi lingliziyya?

Feen nsh-TAIR-ree kee-TAB tahbk MAHG-rah-bee bee ling-glee-ZEE-yah?

And, of course, the following phrases also are useful to know.

WHERE IS THE RESTROOM?

Feen attwalette?

Feen et-twal-ETTE?

MAY I HAVE THE CHECK, PLEASE?

Al-hsab, allah ykhalleek?

El-hiss-AB ahl-LAH ee-hall-LEEK?

DO YOU ACCEPT CREDIT CARDS? TRAVELERS CHECKS?

Wash yumkin ndfa' bi carte credite? Bi sheeka?

Wahsh YOOM-kin nid-FAH bee kart kreh-DEET? Bee SHEE-kah?

Menu Guide

Two alphabetical listings of menu items are provided in this *Guide*. The first is an extensive compilation of menu entries in transliterated Moroccan Arabic (the Moroccan conversational dialect) with English translations, to make ordering food easier. It includes typical Moroccan dishes as well as specialties characteristic of the different regions of the country. Classic regional dishes of Morocco that should not be missed are labeled "regional classic" in the margin next to the menu entry. Some noteworthy dishes popular throughout much of the country—also not to be missed—are labeled "national favorite." Comments on some of our favorites also are included in the margin. The second list of menu items, also with notes in the margin, is in French with English translations. Both lists are cross referenced.

Traditional Moroccan cuisine is enjoyed in several types of establishments ranging from simple roadside cafés to upscale restaurants that have been converted from palatial private residences. Restaurants primarily exist to serve foreign visiters, because most Moroccans prefer to follow cultural tradition and take their meals at home with their families.

French is the most common language on menus. French is still widely spoken in Morocco and is taught at an early age in the schools—a legacy of the 44-year French occupancy in the first half of the 20th century. This, coupled with the fact that the largest group of tourists are from France, makes it a practical choice to use French on menus. The names of some dishes in French are a mixture of French and transliterated Moroccan Arabic. Quotation marks set apart the Moroccan Arabic component. It is becoming more common to see the names of dishes on menus in English and, to some extent, in transliterated Moroccan Arabic as well. Eateries without menus or with their daily offerings posted on a sign will also be encountered.

The transliteration of Moroccan Arabic words is quite problematic. Two disparate systems exist. One is the standardized scheme professional linguists use. The other is a non-standard one, and includes a diverse collection of phonetic spellings for any given word. This guidebook includes spellings from both sources: those based on the transliteration system of Richard Harrell and colleagues (Georgetown University), and others used in such resources as menus, cookbooks and culinary literature. A few Berber culinary terms are also included in the list.

Some symbols used in this guidebook will be unfamiliar to most readers. Several transliterated words contain a consonant called ^cein (^cain) that is not used in English. It represents a gutteral sound that is made far back in the mouth, as in "baa" of a sheep. Common ways to write this consonant in English are with a superscripted c (^c), as used here, or a reverse apostrophe ('). The ^c can be found anywhere within a word. In this *Guide* and in the *Foods & Flavors Guide,* the ^c is ignored when alphabetizing.

The regular apostrophe (') is used in this list to indicate that a vowel between consonants has been dropped. An example is *b'stila* versus *bestila.* Some writers also use the regular apostrophe to symbolize the ^cein and to denote the infrequent glottal stop in Moroccan Arabic, which commonly is described as the sound made between the two vowels in the exclamation "uh oh!" This inconsistency in transliterations can be confusing. In this *Guide* and in the *Foods & Flavors Guide,* the apostrophe is ignored when alphabetizing.

In general, the definite and indefinite articles, which are prefixed to nouns and adjectives by hyphens, are not included. They follow complex rules and are unnecessary for our purposes. For pronunciation aids, see *Helpful Phrases,* p. 75. Also see the *Bibliography,* p. 133, for references to the Moroccan Arabic grammar text and the Moroccan Arabic/English and English/Moroccan Arabic dictionaries written or edited by Richard S. Harrell and Harvey Sobelman.

Moroccans begin their day with a light breakfast (*ftur*), which, at a minimum, consists of bread, butter and preserves, and perhaps some yogurt. Additional dough-based items enjoyed at this time of the day include a family of flat breakfast pastries (*rghaif*) and a pancake (*beghrir*) cooked on one side only, which has little holes on the uncooked side. Street vendors sell pieces of flat, unleavened Berber bread (*harsha*) and deep-fried, sugared doughnuts (*sfinge*). French-style croissants are commonplace. Some hotels offer an assortment of these traditional breakfast items along with the standard Western fare of eggs and cereal. Lunch (*gda*) is the main meal of the day. The most typical dishes are stews (*tagine*) and couscous (*seksu*). Hardly a table in Morocco will be without a preparation of couscous on Friday, the Islamic Sabbath. Like breakfast, supper (^c*sha*) is a light meal. The ever popular *harira,* a soup of lamb or meatballs, lentils, chickpeas, tomatoes and onions, will be the primary focus of this repast. Mint tea will be enjoyed with all meals.

TOP *Tagine lham bil khodra,* lamb stew with seasonal vegetables, served at a roadside eatery near Zagora. **MIDDLE** Assortment of divine pastries, made by master chef/teacher Elkifly Najah and her culinary staff at the Ecole Hôtelière in Fès. **BOTTOM** *Seksu tafaya,* lamb couscous with caramelized onions and raisins, served at the Fint restaurant in Ouarzazate.

TOP LEFT Exuberant fruit and vegetable vendor in Tangier. **TOP RIGHT** El Baraka restaurant, one of several eateries in the narrow, winding passageways of the medina in Chaouen. **BOTTOM** Bread seller at the weekly outdoor market (*souk*) in Khemisset.

TOP LEFT *Shar‘riya medfoun,* lamb stew buried in a nest of steamed vermicelli, made by chef de cuisine Futim-Zohra Oaehdoghini at the Fint restaurant in Ouarzazate. **TOP RIGHT** *Tagine lham tafaya,* lamb stew with caramelized onions, raisins and almonds, served at the Raihani restaurant in Tangier. **MIDDLE** *Seksu* Beidaoui, classic Casablanca-style dish of couscous with seven vegetables, served at Les Remparts restaurant in Fès. **BOTTOM** Mixed lamb and beef *kababs,* served at the Raihani restaurant in Tangier.

TOP *Trid,* stacked crêpes with sauce between them and tasty saffron-flavored chicken on top, prepared by chef de cuisine Naima Amouri at the Palais Salam Hotel in Taroudant. **MIDDLE** *Tagine lham bil berquq wa luz,* lamb stew with prunes and almonds, prepared by chef de cuisine Fatna Kotni at the Dar Marjana restaurant in Marrakech. **BOTTOM** *Harira,* a thick, hearty soup with lamb, lentils, chickpeas, tomatoes and onions, served at the Basmane restaurant in Casablanca.

TOP LEFT Making couscous granules (*seksu*) the traditional way by hand-rolling coarse and very fine semolina flour moistened with water. **TOP RIGHT** Zohra El Meterfi, chef de cuisine at the Palais la Medina restaurant in Fès, making a sheet of *warka,* an ultrathin composite of small, overlapping circles of pastry dough cooked on a special pan (*tobsil dial warka*). **BOTTOM** Cooked sheet of pastry dough (*warka*) for the classic dish of squab pie (*bestila*), made by a pastry specialist at the Yacout restaurant in Marrakech.

TOP *Tagine lham bil khodra* Fassi, Fès-style lamb stew with seasonal vegetables, prepared by Zohra El Meterfi, chef de cuisine at the Palais la Medina restaurant in Fès. **MIDDLE** Chaouen-style couscous (*seksu*) with chickpeas and raisins, served at El Baraka restaurant in Chaouen. **BOTTOM** *Tagine bil hut,* stewed fish in *chermula,* the classic fish marinade, prepared by sous chef Kamel Hassan at the El Korsan restaurant in the El Minzah hotel in Tangier.

TOP LEFT Vendor selling fresh spearmint. Moroccans typically add sprigs of spearmint and chunks of sugar cut from a large loaf to steeping tea. **TOP RIGHT** Serving freshly brewed tea by raising the teapot high above the table, and gracefully and dramatically pouring into small glasses set on a tray. **BOTTOM** Stews being cooked to order for vendors in the Jemaa R'mat market (*souk*) in the Ourika Valley near Marrakech. Some vendors bring their own ingredients and have their midday meal cooked for them.

TOP LEFT *Djaj m'qualli bil hamd marked wa zitun,* chicken stew with preserved lemons and olives, made by Jean-Marc Varin, executive chef of El Mansour restaurant in the Hotel Meridien Tour Hassan in Rabat.
MIDDLE LEFT Individual-size squab pies (*bestila*), prepared by chef de cuisine Haja Fatema at the Palais Mnebhi restaurant in Fès. **RIGHT** An assortment of salads served at Les Remparts restaurant in Fès.
BOTTOM *Tagine lham tafaya,* lamb stew with honey-sweetened garnish, almonds and hard-boiled eggs.

By and large the food served to foreign visitors in restaurants consists of about a dozen well-known special-occasion dishes including those developed in yesteryear's royal kitchens. Within a short time travelers begin to tire of the repetition. Unfortunately, everyday dishes are considered too mundane to be offered as restaurant fare. One among countless possible menu additions is the dish of *byesar* (*bessara, bisar, bisara*), a hearty, thick, Berber dish of puréed broad (fava) beans topped with some paprika, cumin and a drizzle of oil. Served in some nice restaurant crockery, this modest yet delicious soup would be no less impressive than the French classic *potage* St. Germain, which is made with peas.

We hope our many conversations with culinary professionals in Moroccan restaurants and cooking schools about expanding the menu selection will have some influence. Until there is a change, foreign visitors are unlikely to have the opportunity to sample the culinary repertoire of everyday dishes— unless they dine in the markets (*souks*) or in homes with hosts willing to serve everyday fare to guests. If a genuine invitation to join a family for a meal is offered, travelers would do well to accept it (see *Preface,* for one such meal enjoyed by the author). Other possibilities for cultural (and culinary) enrichment are through membership in organizations such as Servas and The Friendship Force (see *Resources,* p. 71).

Travelers invited for a meal with a Moroccan family will be impressed with the hospitality. Seated on couches with a small, round table in front of them, diners partake in the ritual of hand washing before the first dish is brought to the table. This is repeated at the end of the meal. Warm water is poured over the hands from a brass kettle (*tass*) and collected in a copper basin. After the hands are dried, the palms are sprinkled with orange-flower water. The host then utters *"Bismillah,"* which means "with the blessing of God" and also implies that the guests are to enjoy the repast, which can be quite lavish in families of means. Moroccans eat with their right hand, using bread as a utensil. Silverware will be present for visitors, but try eating the Moroccan way—without it! The meal begins with an assortment of cold and hot vegetable salads, along with some crusty wedges or pieces of Moroccan bread. Next is likely to be an elaborate pie (*bestila*) filled with squab or chicken, a lemony egg sauce and sweetened, toasted almonds. This is followed by one or more stews and then a savory couscous dish (*seksu*) topped with meat and vegetables, which is served with some broth to keep it moist. If you haven't paced yourself, you might be too full to eat any! The meal ends with a heaping platter of seasonal fruit and several glasses of mint tea.

Menu Items in Transliterated Moroccan Arabic

REGIONAL CLASSIC   **amlou (amlu; amalu; amalou)** spread made of ground almonds, honey and *argan* oil, a nutty-flavored, edible oil used in the southwestern region of Morocco (see *Foods & Flavors Guide*). See recipe, p. 67.

REGIONAL CLASSIC   **ᶜasidah** thick soup or porridge made from barley grits. It is formed into balls and eaten with butter and honey.

ᶜasir del barba fresh beet juice.

ᶜasir del ᶜineb fresh grape juice.

ᶜasir del romman pomegranate juice.

ᶜasir romman bil limun fresh pomegranate and orange juice.

NATIONAL FAVORITE   **atay b'naᶜ-naᶜ** mint-flavored tea, typically made with green tea. Sprigs of fresh spearmint (*Mentha viridis*) and chunks of sugar cut from a large loaf of sugar are added to the teapot while the tea is brewing. It typically is poured rather dramatically from a teapot held high over a glass.

azenbu Berber dish of seasoned porridge or couscous prepared from grain other than wheat. The porridge often is made with barley grits, and oil is drizzled on top. In the south, *argan* oil is used (see *Foods & Flavors Guide*).

baddaz type of couscous made with cornmeal. Boiled greens are chopped and mixed with the couscous. The dish also may contain meat. Other names for *baddaz* are *dshisha belbula* and *dshisha dial dra.*

baddaz bil hut cornmeal couscous with fish.

baha steamed lamb.

NATIONAL FAVORITE   **bakoola (bakoula, bekkula, beqqula)** name for wild greens or a salad of steamed and sautéed wild greens. Mallow, a nutritious spinach-like plant with large leaves, typically is used. Chard is substituted when mallow is out of season. Other favorite substitutes are spinach and purslane.

bakoola (bakoula, bekkula, beqqula) bil hamd marked wa zitun salad of steamed and sautéed wild greens with olives and preserved lemons. See p. 43 for a recipe with Swiss chard as a substitute for the commonly used mallow.

bakoola (bakoula, bekkula, beqqula) bil zitun salad of steamed and sautéed wild greens with olives. See p. 42 for recipe with spinach as a substitute for the commonly used mallow.

baraka word meaning divine power or luck. This word will be encountered often, even as the name of a restaurant (see color insert).

batata hluwa bil kamun wa skinjbir sweet-potato salad with cumin and ginger.

bdenshal meqli fried eggplant.

beghrir yeast-raised semolina pancake cooked on one side only, without oil, in a round, unglazed earthenware dish. The "uncooked," upper side is full of little holes. The pancake traditionally is enjoyed for breakfast, and more recently, as a dessert, with melted butter and honey or sugar. **NATIONAL FAVORITE**

bekkula (bakoola, bakoula, beqqula) name for wild greens or a salad of steamed and sautéed wild greens. Mallow, a nutritious spinach-like plant with large leaves, typically is used. Chard is substituted when mallow is out of season. Other favorite substitutes are spinach and purslane. **NATIONAL FAVORITE**

bekkula (bakoola, bakoula, beqqula) bil hamd marked wa zitun salad of steamed and sautéed wild greens with olives and preserved lemon. See p. 43 for a recipe with Swiss chard as a substitute for the commonly used mallow.

bekkula (bakoola, bakoula, beqqula) bil zitun salad of steamed and sautéed wild greens with olives. See p. 42 for a recipe with spinach as a substitute for the commonly used mallow.

berkukesh (birkukis) dish of large (3 mm or greater) couscous granules (*mhammsa*) cooked in milk.

besbas methun fennel purée.

besla m'assala spiced onions with honey.

bessara (bisar, bisara, byesar) hearty, thick, Berber dish of puréed broad (fava) beans topped with some paprika, cumin and a drizzle of oil. It is breakfast street food and resembles hummus, which is made of chickpeas. In Marrakech and the surrounding countryside markets, it typically is cooked in characteristic round-bottomed, earthenware crocks with flared rims. These cooking vessels sit at an angle on a charcoal burner to facilitate removal of their contents with a long-handled ladle. **NATIONAL FAVORITE**

bestila (b'stila, besteeya) large and elaborate festive pie served as the first course in a *diffa,* or celebration feast. It is made with many ultrathin, round sheets of pastry dough called *warka,* and typically filled with pieces of cooked squab (often with bones), a lemony egg sauce and sweetened, toasted almonds. The more traditional squab filling may be replaced with chicken. See *Foods & Flavors Guide* for details on assembling pie. **NATIONAL FAVORITE**

bestila bil djaj variation of the festive pie called *bestila*. It is made with chicken instead of squab.

bestila bil hut **bestila** variation of the festive pie called *bestila*. It contains fish in a marinade called *chermula* (see *Foods & Flavors Guide*), which is a mixture of tomatoes, onion, garlic, cumin, paprika, hot red pepper, cilantro and flat-leaf parsley.

DELICIOUS **bestila bil ruz** variation of the festive pie called *bestila*. It contains a rice filling that is flavored with almonds and orange-flower water. The dish can be a first course or a dessert.

bibi m^cammar stuffed turkey.

birkukis (berkukesh) dish of large (3 mm or greater) couscous granules (*mhammsa*) cooked in milk.

NATIONAL FAVORITE **bisar (bessara, bisara, byesar)** hearty, thick, Berber dish of puréed broad (fava) beans topped with some paprika, cumin and a drizzle of oil. It is breakfast street food and resembles hummus, which is made of chickpeas. In Marrakech and the surrounding countryside markets, it typically is cooked in characteristic round-bottomed, earthenware crocks with flared rims. These cooking vessels sit at an angle on a charcoal burner to facilitate removal of their contents with a long-handled ladle.

NATIONAL FAVORITE **boulfaf (bu-lfaf)** type of kebab in which pieces of fresh lamb's liver seasoned with cumin, paprika and cayenne are individually wrapped in sheep's caul, put on skewers and grilled over charcoal. *Bu-lfaf* is one of the traditional lamb dishes eaten during ^cId le-Kbir (Aid el Kebir), the four-day religious festival that includes the sacrifice of a lamb. (Fr. *brochettes de foie*)

bousaif bil chermula braised swordfish seasoned with *chermula,* the classic "dry" marinade for fish. See recipe, p. 61.

braniya stew of lamb named for the fried eggplant that garnishes it.

NATIONAL FAVORITE **brik** savory filled pastry, usually containing eggs. It is of Tunisian origin.

briwat (briouat) bil bid pastry triangles filled with eggs and herbs.

briwat (briouat) bil fakya pastry triangles filled with dried fruit.

briwat (briouat) bil kefta pastry triangles filled with minced meat.

FABULOUS **briwat (briouat) bil luz** pastry triangles filled with almond paste. See recipe, p. 62.

briwat (briouat) bil merguez cigar-shaped pastries filled with small beef or lamb sausages heavily seasoned with paprika and cayenne pepper, which give the sausage a reddish color, along with black pepper and garlic. (Fr. *"briouat" aux "merguez"*)

briwat (briouat) bil mohk pastry triangles filled with brains. (Fr. *"briouat" à la cervelle*)

briwat (briouat) bil qemrun pastry triangles filled with shrimp and vermicelli.   TASTY

briwat (briouat) bil ruz pastry triangles filled with sweetened rice (Fr. *"briouat" au riz*).

briwat (briouat) el-bestila pastry triangles containing the squab, egg and almond filling used to make *bestila*.

b'stila (bestila, besteeya) large and elaborate festive pie served as   NATIONAL FAVORITE
the first course of a *diffa,* or celebration feast. It is made with many ultrathin, round sheets of pastry dough called *warka,* and typically is filled with pieces of cooked squab (often with bones), a lemony egg sauce and sweetened, toasted almonds. The more traditional squab filling may be replaced with chicken. See *Foods & Flavors Guide* for details on assembling pie.

btata m'qualli potatoes cooked with parsley, garlic, ginger and saffron.

buboinott (bubanett) large (about 3-inch diameter), foot-long sausage filled with organ meat. In Rabat it is a sausage made with lamb tripe.

bu-lfaf (boulfaf) type of kebab in which pieces of fresh lamb's   NATIONAL FAVORITE
liver seasoned with cumin, paprika and cayenne are individually wrapped in sheep's caul, put on skewers and grilled over charcoal. *Bu-lfaf* is one of the traditional lamb dishes eaten during ᶜId le-Kbir (Aid el Kebir), the four-day religious festival that includes the sacrifice of a lamb. (Fr. *brochettes de foie*)

buzrug (buzruq) bil matisha mussels with tomatoes and cilantro.

byesar (bessara, bisar, bisara) hearty, thick, Berber dish of   NATIONAL FAVORITE
puréed broad (fava) beans topped with some paprika, cumin and a drizzle of oil. It is breakfast street food that resembles hummus, which is made of chickpeas. In Marrakech and the surrounding countryside markets, it typically is cooked in characteristic round-bottomed, earthenware crocks with flared rims. These cooking vessels sit at an angle on a charcoal burner to facilitate removal of their contents with a long-handled ladle.

chakchouka (tektuka) cold tomato and sweet pepper salad. The   NATIONAL FAVORITE
dish is named after the bubbling sound of the mixture of seasoned chopped tomatoes in oil as it simmers and reduces to a purée without water. It is a popular Sephardic dish of Algerian/Tunisian origin.

cha^c^riya (sha^c^riya) **bahara** steamed vermicelli with sugar and cinnamon.

NATIONAL FAVORITE cha^c^riya (sha^c^riya) **medfoun** nest of steamed vermicelli with stewed meat hidden within it. Also simply called *medfoun*. See recipe, p. 47.

NATIONAL FAVORITE **chebbakiya (shebbakiya)** very sweet leavened pastry resembling an irregular coil of ribbons. It is made of dough flavored with orange-flower water and saffron. The dough is rolled out, then cut into ribbons that are deep-fried, dipped in hot honey and sprinkled with toasted sesame seeds. These pastries are the usual accompaniment to *harira,* the soup eaten at sundown each day during the month-long fast of Ramadan, although they are also enjoyed, with or without *harira,* any day of the year. *Chebbakiya* is also the name of another pastry made from the same dough, which is piped through a funnel or a pastry bag and formed into rosettes on the surface of the boiling oil. The rosettes are similarly dunked in hot oil and covered with toasted sesame seeds. These pastries are also called *halwa chebbakiya (shebbakiya)* and *mahalkra.*

WONDERFUL **chlada (shlada) bil barba wa ma zher** grated beet salad flavored with orange-flower water.

chlada (shlada) bil felfel salad or condiment made with minced tomatoes, cucumbers, onions and hot red chile peppers dressed in oil and vinegar.

chlada (shlada) bil felfel wa hamd marked salad of roasted peppers and preserved lemons.

chlada (shlada) bil ful wa zitun salad with fava beans and olives.

chlada (shlada) bil matisha wa besla tomato and onion salad or condiment typically accompanying grilled meat and fish.

chlada (shlada) felfel meshwi grilled pepper salad.

chlada (shlada) khizu carrot salad.

NATIONAL FAVORITE **chlada (shlada) limun** orange salad flavored with cinnamon and orange-flower water. See recipe, p. 46. (Fr. *salade d'orange à la cannelle*)

chlada (shlada) matisha wa na^c^-na^c^ chopped tomatoes flavored with mint.

GREAT CHOICE **chlada (shlada) meshwi (mechoui)** salad of roasted tomatoes and green peppers marinated in vinegar and oil.

chorba bil dshisha soup made with crushed grains of wheat. (Fr. *soupe de "dchicha" au blé*)

chorba bil ful Passover soup of fava beans flavored with cilantro. It is a dish on the Moroccan Jewish menu. (Moroccan cuisine is enriched by the many contributions made by Jews who settled in Morocco following their exile from Spain after the fall of Granada in 1492.)

chorba bil hamus chickpea soup.

chorba bil khodra vegetable soup flavored with saffron.　　　GOOD CHOICE

choua steamed mutton. (Fr. *viande de mouton à la vapeur*)

dafina one-dish Moroccan stew for the Jewish Sabbath. *Dafina,* made midday on Friday, used to be cooked uninterrupted in the embers of a public oven until the same time on the following day. It is often flavored with mace and typically contains beans or chickpeas, potatoes and meat. *Dafina* may also include eggs, which cook in the shell, or dumplings (*kouclas*) made of rice or bread that are cooked in a foil or cheesecloth bag placed in the middle of the pot. Also called *scheena,* and less commonly, *frackh.* (Moroccan cuisine is enriched by the many contributions made by Jews who settled in Morocco following their exile from Spain after the fall of Granada in 1492.)

der^ciya bil zitun wa matisha baked sea perch with olives and tomatoes.

^cdes bil ger^ca hamra wa khlii lentils with pumpkin and spice-cured, sun-dried strips of beef. (Fr. *lentilles au courges et "khlii"*)

^cdes bil khlii lentils with spice-cured, sun-dried strips of beef. (Fr. *lentilles au "khlii"*)

^cdes bil selq lentils with Swiss chard.

djaj besla chicken with onions.

djaj bil ^cassal wa romman wa luz chicken with honey, pomegranate　　　GREAT juice and toasted almonds. See p. 59 for recipe using cornish hens instead of chicken.

djaj bil berquq chicken with prunes. It is a specialty of Chaouen, a city in the Rif Mountains area.

djaj bil bid wa luz chicken with eggs and almonds.

djaj bil ger^ca hamra chicken with pumpkin.

djaj bil luz wa jben chicken with almonds and cheese.

djaj bil ma^cdnus chicken with onion and parsley.

djaj bil ruz chicken with rice.

djaj bil ruz wa limun chicken with rice and lemon.　　　DELICIOUS

djaj bil tmer chicken with dates. See recipe, p. 58.

djaj bil zbib chicken with raisins.

djaj bil zitun meslalla chicken with cracked green olives. (Fr. *poulet "meslalla"*)

djaj bil zitun wa lim chicken with olives and lime.

djaj k'dra bil besla chicken with chickpeas and onions, flavored with saffron and paprika. (Fr. *poulet "k'dra" aux pois chiches et aux oignons*)

djaj k'dra bil luz wa ruz chicken with almonds and rice in a buttery sauce with onions, pepper and saffron.

REGIONAL CLASSIC **djaj k'dra touimiya** chicken with chickpeas and almonds in a buttery sauce with onions, pepper and saffron. It is a specialty of Essaouira.

djaj m^cammar bil k'seksu chicken stuffed with couscous. (Fr. *poulet "m^cammar" farci au couscous*)

DIVINE **djaj matisha m'sla** stew of lamb or chicken in a sauce of honey-sweetened tomatoes. (Fr. *poulet aux tomates et au miel*)

djaj m'chermel chicken with olives and preserved lemons in a creamy sauce flavored with ginger, paprika, saffron, cumin and cilantro. Also called *tagine djaj m'chermel*.

djaj mefenned braised, browned whole chicken encrusted with a seasoned egg mixture.

djaj meshwi (mechoui) roasted chicken.

GREAT CHOICE **djaj m'hammer** stew of braised, browned chicken in a buttery sauce flavored with paprika and cumin.

djaj m'kaddem stew of chicken cooked in a sauce flavored with saffron, flat-leaf parsley and cinnamon. Before serving the stew, a mixture of beaten eggs seasoned with cumin is added, which, when cooked, makes the dish omelet-like. Also called *djaj souiri*. (Fr. *poulet aux oeufs*)

djaj m'qualli stew of chicken flavored with ginger and saffron. (Fr. *poulet "m'qualli"*)

NATIONAL FAVORITE **djaj m'qualli bil hamd marked wa zitun** stew of chicken with olives and preserved lemons in a sauce flavored with ginger and saffron. See recipes, pp. 56–58. (Fr. *poulet "m'qualli" au citron comfit*)

djaj souiri stew of chicken cooked in a sauce flavored with saffron, flat-leaf parsley and cinnamon. Before serving the stew, a mixture of beaten eggs seasoned with cumin is added, which, when cooked, makes the dish omelet-like. Also called *djaj m'kaddem*. (Fr. *poulet aux oeufs*)

djaj tarat vegetable dish of potatoes, chickpeas and onions, flavored with *smen* (aged butter), saffron and cilantro, cooked until just a light sauce is left. It is served in individual dishes. There is no chicken in this preparation despite its name. It is said that the fowl meant for this dish flew away and that is how *djaj tarat* became a vegetarian offering.

douara stew of lamb giblets (heart, liver and tripe) from a freshly NATIONAL FAVORITE killed sheep in a hot sauce of tomatoes, onions, garlic, paprika, cayenne and cumin. It is a traditional dish eaten during ᶜId le-Kbir (Aid el Kebir), the four-day religious festival that includes the sacrifice of a lamb.

dshisha dish of seasoned porridge or couscous prepared with wheat or barley grits.

dshisha dial dra type of couscous made with cornmeal. Boiled greens are chopped and mixed with the couscous. The dish also may contain meat. Other names for *dshisha dial dra* are *dshisha belbula* and *baddaz.*

dshisha sikuk couscous made with barley grits and fava beans.

fackasch small, flat, yeast-raised round of sweet bread flavored with aniseed, caraway and poppyseed.

feggus (feqqus) wa matisha b'naᶜ-naᶜ salad of cucumbers and tomatoes flavored with mint.

felalia thick, light-yellow soup or porridge made with barley and REGIONAL CLASSIC laced with thin strips cut from leaves of a wild plant. It is a specialty of the Tafilalt area.

feqqas (fekkas) twice-baked, biscotti-like cookies flavored with NATIONAL FAVORITE anise and sesame seeds. Raisins and almonds are often added. To make them, quarter-inch thick rounds are cut from a partially baked cylinder of dough and baked again. See recipe, p. 65.

frach mᶜammar bil k'seksu squab stuffed with couscous.

frackh one-dish Moroccan stew for the Jewish Sabbath. *Frackh,* made midday on Friday, used to be cooked uninterrupted in the embers of a public oven until the same time on the following day. It is often flavored with mace and typically contains beans or chickpeas, potatoes and meat. *Frackh* may also include eggs, which cook in the shell, or dumplings (*kouclas*) made of rice or bread that are cooked in a foil or cheesecloth bag placed in the middle of the pot. Also called *dafina* and *scheena.* (Moroccan cuisine is enriched by the many contributions made by Jews who settled in Morocco following their exile from Spain after the fall of Granada in 1492.)

fwad tripe stew.

gerᶜa hamra sweet pumpkin purée.

gernina (garnina) meat stew flavored with pale-green stems of REGIONAL CLASSIC the wild thistle, which are notoriously difficult to trim of tough parts. It is a specialty of Fés. (Fr. *tajine aux côtes de chardons*)

NATIONAL FAVORITE **ghoriba (griyba)** rich, buttery semolina cookie with a crinkled, macaroon-like surface dusted with powdered sugar. Some versions are made with regular flour and are more like short-bread. Crushed, toasted sesame seeds or finely minced almonds may be added to the dough. Butter flavored with a marijuana extract is sometimes added to homemade cookies. See recipe for (drug-free) cookies, p. 66. A peanut cookie similar to *ghoriba* is called *penaga*.

halwa dial jenjlan squares of honeyed sesame seeds and ground almonds.

NATIONAL FAVORITE **halwa shebbakiya (chebbakiya)** very sweet leavened pastry resembling an irregular coil of ribbons. It is made of dough flavored with orange-flower water and saffron that is deep-fried, dipped in hot honey and sprinkled with toasted sesame seeds. These pastries are the usual accompaniment to *harira,* the soup eaten at sundown each day during the month-long fast of Ramadan, although they are also enjoyed, with or without *harira,* any day of the year. *Halwa shebbakiya* is also the name of another pastry made from the same dough, which is piped through a funnel or a pastry bag and formed into rosettes on the surface of the boiling oil. The rosettes are similarly dunked in hot oil and covered with toasted sesame seeds. These pastries are also called *shebbakiya (chebbakiya)* and *mahalkra.*

NATIONAL FAVORITE **harira** traditional, hearty soup made with lamb or meatballs, lentils, chickpeas, tomatoes and onions, flavored with saffron and cilantro. There are many regional variations. See recipe, p. 41. Just before serving, it is thickened with *tedouira,* a mixture of yeast or flour and water that sometimes is allowed to ferment slightly first. Beaten eggs can also be added. The soup invariably is served at sundown each day during the month-long fast of Ramadan, but can be enjoyed any day of the year. *Harira* is eaten with a ladle-like, hand-carved spoon called *mgerfa (mgorfa)* made from lemon or orange wood. Typical soup accompaniments are dates or sweet pastries called *shebbakiya,* which resemble irregular coils of ribbons.

harira kerwiya lemon-flavored mint and caraway soup that traditionally is served with lamb's head in the morning.

REGIONAL CLASSIC **harira Mrakchiya** Marrakech-style meatless soup with kidney beans, rice and coriander, flavored with paprika.

harissa hot sauce of Tunisian origin made with dried chile peppers, garlic and oil. It is served on the side with many dishes.

harsha large rounds of fried, flat, dense bread made of semolina. The rounds are cut into pieces and typically enjoyed with tea at breakfast, or on the run in the early morning (see *Foods & Flavors Guide*).

helwa rhifa special-occasion cake made with thin sheets of fried dough. The sheets are crumbled, mixed with honey that has been heated with orange-flower water and formed into a cone shape. It is crowned with a dollop of butter.

herbil porridge made with coarsely ground hard wheat cooked in milk and flavored with orange-flower water.

hergma stew of lamb's trotters with coarsely ground wheat, chickpeas and onions, flavored with paprika and cayenne. It is one of several traditional dishes made with the lamb sacrificed for ᶜId le-Kbir (Aid el Kebir). This four-day great Festival of Sacrifice, held 50 days after Ramadan, commemorates God's will that the Prophet Abraham sacrifice a lamb rather than his son Isaac. **NATIONAL FAVORITE**

hleb bil luz beverage of sweetened milk and pulverized almonds, flavored with orange-flower water. It often is served with dates.

hut bil chermula fried or baked fish, seasoned with a dry marinade likely to contain onion, garlic, cilantro, flat-leaf parsley, saffron, paprika, hot red pepper and cumin.

hut mᶜammar bil ruz fish stuffed with rice. (Fr. *poisson farci au riz*)

hut mᶜammar bil selq fish stuffed with Swiss chard.

hut meqli fried fish.

hut meshwi (mechoui) roasted fish.

hut m'qualli *tagine* of fish in a sauce flavored with ginger and saffron and garnished with preserved lemons. (Fr. *poisson en tajine "m'qualli"*) **NATIONAL FAVORITE**

jaban nougat-like candy. It is a specialty of Fès. Vendors in the medina display large blocks of it, which they cut into slices. **REGIONAL CLASSIC**

kabab (kebab) pieces of meat or giblets, and often pieces of fat, broiled on a skewer. Moroccan kebabs will not have vegetables such as tomatoes, peppers, onions or mushrooms threaded on the skewer between the meat or giblets. See recipe, p. 55. (Fr. *brochettes*) **NATIONAL FAVORITE**

kabab maghdour (megdur) stew of bone-in or boneless lamb cooked with onions, cumin and paprika. The name of the dish means "cheating" kebabs, acknowledgment of the fact that the meat has not been grilled on skewers. (Fr. *tajine de "kabab maghdour"*)

kabab maghdour (megdur) bil bid stew of bone-in or boneless lamb cooked with onions, cumin and paprika, with eggs poached in the sauce just before serving. (Fr. *tajine de "kabab maghdour" aux oeufs*)

NATIONAL FAVORITE **ka°b el ghzal** crescent-shaped pastries called "gazelle's horns," which are filled with almond paste. Only a very thin shell of pastry encases the filling. Orange-flower water is added to the dough and often to the almond paste as well. See recipe, p. 64. (Fr. *cornes de gazelle*)

ka°b el ghzal m'fenned variety of the crescent-shaped pastries called "gazelle's horns" that are dipped in orange-flower water and coated with powdered sugar.

REGIONAL CLASSIC **kamama** sweet lamb stew seasoned with ginger. It is dressed with onion rings cooked in *smen* and olive oil, and flavored with saffron and cinnamon. *Kamama* is a specialty of Meknès. (Fr. *tajine de viande aux oignons*)

REGIONAL CLASSIC **kanaria (qennariya)** stew flavored with stalks of the domesticated thistle plant, or cardoon (*Cynara cardunculus*), a relative of the globe artichoke. The stalks are trimmed of leaves, thorns, and tough fibers, cut into small pieces and cooked with meat and preserved lemons. It is a specialty of Fès.

kebda liver salad.

kefta grilled minced lamb with spices.

NATIONAL FAVORITE **kefta bil matisha wa bid** stew of meatballs in a tomato-based sauce with onions and garlic, and seasoned with paprika, cumin and cayenne pepper. Eggs are poached in the sauce in the cooking dish just before serving, and appear nestled between the meatballs. Also called *tagine kabab maghdour (megdur) bil bid* and *kefta mkaouara*. See recipe, p. 48. (Fr. *boulettes de "kefta" aux oeufs*)

kefta bil ruz meatballs with rice.

kefta kabab (kebab) minced lamb with spices, grilled on skewers. (Fr. *brochettes de viande hachée*)

kefta Mrakchiya stuffed meatballs with dried fruit in sweet onion sauce. It is a specialty of Marrakech.

kefta m'chermal meatballs in a sauce with onions, flat-leaf parsley and cilantro, flavored with ginger, cumin, paprika and saffron.

kefta mkaouara stew of meatballs in a tomato-based sauce with onions and garlic, and seasoned with paprika, cumin and cayenne pepper. Eggs are poached in the sauce in the cooking dish just before serving, and appear nestled between the meatballs. Also called *kefta bil matisha wa bid* and *tagine kabab maghdour (megdur) bil bid*. See recipe, p. 48. (Fr. *boulettes de "kefta" aux oeufs*)

keneffa sweet dessert *bestila* made of stacked rounds of fried **FABULOUS** *warka* (paper-thin pastry). Between the pastry layers is a thickened almond-milk mixture flavored with orange-flower water. Sometimes confectioner's cream flavored with orange-flower water is put between the pastry layers. Coarsely chopped almonds coated with cinnamon and sugar are sprinkled on the cream or thickened milk before another pastry layer is added. The top pastry layer is decorated with powdered sugar and stripes of cinnamon. This dessert is a specialty of Marrakech.

kesra Moroccan bread—a soft-crusted round, flattened loaf. Moroccans traditionally eat from a communal bowl with their right hand, using a piece of bread as a utensil. This dense, absorbent bread is perfect for scooping up food and soaking up delicious sauces. The addition of aniseed and sesame seeds to the bread is usually reserved for loaves made for celebrations. Moroccan bread is also called *khobz*.

khess bil limun wa tmer lettuce, orange and date salad. **GOOD CHOICE**

khizu bil limun salad of grated carrots and sliced oranges (or orange-flower water) dusted with cinnamon.

khizu mehquq grated carrot salad sweetened with sugar and flavored with orange-flower water.

khizu mrqed carrot salad with cayenne and cumin.

khlii bil bid spice-cured, sun-dried strips of beef with eggs. See **NATIONAL FAVORITE** *Foods & Flavors Guide*. (Fr. *"khlii" aux oeufs*)

khlii bil limun spice-cured, sun-dried strips of beef with lemon. See *Foods & Flavors Guide*. (Fr. *"khlii" au citron*)

khobz Moroccan bread—a soft-crusted round, flattened loaf. Moroccans traditionally eat from a communal bowl with their right hand, using a piece of bread as a utensil. This dense, absorbent bread is perfect for scooping up food and soaking up delicious sauces. The addition of aniseed and sesame seeds to the bread is usually reserved for loaves made for celebrations. Moroccan bread is also called *kesra*.

khobz belbula barley bread.

khobz bil kerwiya whole-wheat rolls with caraway.

khobz bishemar griddle-fried bread stuffed with seasoned fat, which seeps out through holes poked in the dough, providing both flavor and the oil for frying.

khobz meqli skillet-baked semolina flatbread. See recipe, p. 46.

khyar mehquq grated cucumber salad sweetened with sugar and seasoned with *za^ctar,* a wild herb of the thyme and oregano family.

kourien dish of sheep's trotters and chickpeas, flavored with garlic, cumin, paprika and preserved lemon. The preparation may also be sweetened with honey or sugar and have a dash of cinnamon.

krachel aniseed and sesame seed bun.

NATIONAL FAVORITE **k'seksu (seksu)** couscous, Morocco's national dish. There are many different preparations, including sweet ones served for dessert. All have as their basis granules (actually a pasta) of the same name formed from wheat and other grains (see *seksu, Foods & Flavors Guide*), which are piled into a conical mound and topped with meat, vegetables, or cinnamon and sugar. A savory couscous dish traditionally is served for lunch on Friday, the Islamic Sabbath. Savory dishes of couscous often are served with some broth to keep the granules moist.

NATIONAL FAVORITE **kuwa (kouah)** type of kebab with pieces of fresh liver dredged in cumin, paprika and cayenne alternating with pieces of mutton fat on the skewer.

lben buttermilk.

left bil ^cineb braised turnips with raisins.

lernib m'hammer rabbit stewed in a sauce flavored with paprika and cumin, then browned by frying in butter.

NATIONAL FAVORITE **lham bil berquq wa luz** lamb or beef stew with prunes and almonds. See recipe, p. 50. (Fr. *agneau ou boeuf aux pruneaux et aux amandes*)

lham bil gra^c taxrifin wa za^ctar meat with zucchini squash, flavored with *za^ctar,* a wild herb of the thyme and oregano family. (Fr. *tajine de viande aux courgettes*)

WONDERFUL **lham bil quq wa gra^c taxrifin** lamb stew with artichokes and zucchini. See recipe, p. 54. (Fr. *agneau aux artichauts et aux courgettes*)

lham bil slaouia wa mlokhia meat with squash and okra. (Fr. *tajine aux courgettes "slaouia" et "mlokhia"*)

lham bil zitun wa limun meat with olives and preserved lemon.

lham m'hammer lamb (or beef) stewed in a sauce flavored with paprika and cumin, then browned by frying in butter.

lham m'sla meat seasoned with ginger and saffron and cooked in honey and cinnamon until the glaze is dark.

lham sfarjehl m'assala roast lamb with quinces and honey.

lsen m'tayeeb bil luz tongue with almonds.

lubya (lubia, loubia) white kidney bean soup with lamb. ·TASTY·

lubya (lubia, loubia) k'dra popular street dish of white kidney beans, onions and flat-leaf parsley, flavored with saffron.

mahalkra very sweet leavened pastry resembling an irregular coil of ribbons. It is made of dough flavored with orange-flower water and saffron that is deep-fried, dipped in hot honey and sprinkled with toasted sesame seeds. See *halwa shebbakiya* and *shebbakiya (chebbakiya)*, this *Guide*.

ma^cjun small, sesame-seed–coated balls made of a sweet paste of dates, raisins, crushed nuts, honey, butter and spices (especially the complex blend called *ras l-hanut*; see *Foods & Flavors Guide*). Extracts of drugs such as marijuana (or hashish) are sometimes put into homemade *ma^cjun*. These extracts are made by simmering the seeds and stems of the plant in a watery mixture of butter or *smen,* (aged butter; see *Foods & Flavors Guide*). After the mixture cools, the fat solidifies and can be skimmed off the surface, leaving behind the marijuana debris. Today, marijuana-laced homemade *ma^cjun* is more likely to be made by wealthier people, who share some with a close circle of friends.

ma^cjun letshin candied oranges.

ma^cquda omelet.

marak matisha bil mlokhia(mluxiya) stew of tomatoes and okra.

marak selq stew of chard.

matisha m^cammara tomatoes stuffed with grated vegetables.

matisha m'sla tomato purée or jam, sweetened with honey. This   ·REGIONAL CLASSIC· specialty of Fès is used as a sauce with meat or as a preserve. See recipe, p. 45.

mechoui (meshwi) whole lamb spit-roasted over hot embers for   ·NATIONAL FAVORITE· several hours and basted frequently with butter seasoned with garlic, cumin and paprika. When done properly, the meat is juicy and tender, and the skin dark and crispy. Morsels are picked from the roasted lamb with the fingers and dipped in ground cumin and coarse salt. It traditionally is served as part of a banquet that follows a tribal celebration (*moussem*).

medfoun nest of steamed vermicelli with stewed meat hidden   ·NATIONAL FAVORITE· within it. Also called *sha^criya (cha^criya) medfoun*. See recipe, p. 47. A similar dish is made with couscous rather than vermicelli.

melj m'hammer braised and browned leg of lamb in a buttery sauce flavored with paprika and cumin.

melowi (milwi) type of *rghaif* pastry (see *Foods & Flavors Guide*). It is made by taking a thin rectangle of dough, rolling it up like a jellyroll, standing the roll up on one end and squashing the whole thing flat. The pastry is then fried and served with butter and honey.

melowi (milwi) bil khlii thin rectangle of dough topped with crumbled spice-cured, sun-dried strips of beef (*khlii*), rolled up like a jellyroll, tipped on end and then squashed flat and fried.

mescouta date cake.

NATIONAL FAVORITE   **meshwi (mechoui)** whole lamb spit-roasted over hot embers for several hours and basted frequently with butter seasoned with garlic, cumin and paprika. When done properly, the meat is juicy and tender, and the skin dark and crispy. Morsels are picked from the roasted lamb with the fingers and dipped in ground cumin and coarse salt. It traditionally is served as part of a banquet that follows a tribal celebration (*moussem*).

meslalla olive salad.

mezgueldi dish of onion rings and spice-cured, sun-dried strips of beef (*khlii*), seasoned with paprika, chile peppers and parsley.

NATIONAL FAVORITE   **m'hanncha** "the snake," a tight coil of pastry stuffed with almond paste. It is baked until golden, dusted with powdered sugar and decorated with lines drawn with cinnamon. To make *m'hanncha,* sheets of thin pastry dough (*warka*) are wrapped around long "sausages" of almond paste that is flavored with orange-flower water. These wrapped lengths of pastry-encased almond paste are then arranged in a tight coil, beginning at the center of a round baking pan. Several lengths are needed to complete the coil.

NATIONAL FAVORITE   **miklee** a folded and fried unstuffed pastry of the *rghaif* family (see *Foods & Flavors Guide*) named the "judge's ears." It is made by taking a small ball of dough and rolling it into a very thin square, which is then folded into thirds by bringing first one side then the other over the middle section. This process is repeated after rotating the strip 90 degrees, producing a square pastry about 4–5 inches wide and nine layers thick. Before it is fried, the pastry square is stretched on each of its four sides to produce uneven contours. It is eaten with a topping of sugar and cinnamon or with warm honey. Also called *wadnine el kadi.*

mlokhia bil khlii soup-like dish made with spice-cured, sun-dried strips of beef (*khlii*), beans and dried, powdered okra and flavored with paprika. (Fr. *soupe de gombos au "khlii"*)

mohk brain salad.

mͨqoda small, spicy, fried potato dumplings common in the countryside. They are served with bread.

mrouzia rich, sweet and spicy stew of lamb cooked in a buttery sauce with raisins, almonds, cinnamon, nutmeg, garlic, saffron and a spice mixture called *ras l-hanut* (see *Foods & Flavors Guide*). This dish is traditionally served during ⁿId le-Kbir (Aid el Kebir), the four-day religious festival that includes the sacrifice of a lamb.   **NATIONAL FAVORITE**

m'sla bil gerᶜa hamra baked pumpkin with caramelized onions, cinnamon and almonds.

mtsimen type of rghaif pastry (see *Foods & Flavors Guide*). It is made by folding dough into a wedge and griddle-frying it. The pastry is eaten with butter and honey.

nafaᶜ semolina soup flavored with aniseed. (Fr. *soupe de semoule au "nafaᶜ"*)   **TASTY**

penaga peanut cookie similar to the *ghoriba*.

qennariya (kanaria) stew flavored with stalks of the domesticated thistle plant, or cardoon (*Cynara cardunculus*), a relative of the globe artichoke. The stalks are trimmed of leaves, thorns, and tough fibers, cut into small pieces and cooked with meat and preserved lemons. It is a specialty of Fès.   **REGIONAL CLASSIC**

quodban (qetban, qotban) lamb kebabs.   **NATIONAL FAVORITE**

quodban (qetban, qotban) bil hut fish kebabs.

quodban (qetban, qotban) bil kefta lamb meatball kebabs.

quodban (qetban, qotban) Mrakchiya Marrakech-style shish kebabs served in pockets of warmed bread, with a pinch of cumin, some tomato and onion relish and a spoonful of *harissa,* the thick, spicy condiment of Tunisian origin made with dried hot red chile peppers, olive oil and garlic.   **REGIONAL CLASSIC**

quq bil ruz artichoke hearts and rice.

ras mbakhar steamed head, typically lamb or beef. Cheeks and tongue are favorites.

romman jben pomegranate seeds mixed with honey and grated cheese.

roztel kadi version of *rghaif* pastry (see *Foods & Flavors Guide*) named "judge's turban" because of its appearance. The dough is rolled into a fine thread and coiled to make a flat, circular pastry that is fried. It is served with honey and butter.

DELICIOUS **ruz bil hleb** creamy rice pudding flavored with orange-flower water.

sannur bil besla wa ᶜineb conger eel with onions and raisins. It is a specialty of Essaouira.

scheena one-dish Moroccan stew for the Jewish Sabbath. *Scheena,* made midday on Friday, used to be cooked uninterrupted in the embers of a public oven until the same time on the following day. It is often flavored with mace and typically contains beans or chickpeas, potatoes and meat. *Scheena* may also include eggs, which cook in the shell, or dumplings (*kouclas*) made of rice or bread that are cooked in a foil or cheesecloth bag placed in the middle of the pot. Also called *dafina,* and less commonly, *frackh*. (Moroccan cuisine is enriched by the many contributions made by Jews who settled in Morocco following their exile from Spain after the fall of Granada in 1492.)

NATIONAL FAVORITE **seffa (sffa)** sweet dessert of couscous made with fine-granule semolina (*smida*) (see *Foods & Flavors Guide*). The couscous is put on a plate and patted into a cone-shaped mound, which is then decorated with nuts, dried fruit and radial lines of cinnamon running from the top to the bottom of the cone. Powdered sugar crowns the peak. It is served with small bowls of milk or buttermilk. Tea and fruit are served afterwards.

seffa medfoun stew of giblets nestled out of sight within a pile of couscous made with fine granule semolina (*smida*).

NATIONAL FAVORITE **seksu (k'seksu)** couscous, Morocco's national dish. There are many different preparations, including sweet ones served for dessert. All have as their basis granules (actually a pasta) of the same name formed from wheat and other grains (see *seksu, Foods & Flavors Guide*), which are piled into a conical mound and topped with meat, vegetables, or cinnamon and sugar. A savory couscous dish is traditionally served for lunch on Friday, the Islamic Sabbath. Savory dishes of couscous often are served with some broth to keep the grains moist.

NATIONAL FAVORITE **seksu Beidaoui** Casablanca-style couscous with seven different seasonal vegetables and often meat. The vegetables are arranged in radial fashion on a mound of couscous, with the meat on the peak. It is considered good luck to have seven vegetables in the preparation, but more or less than seven also will be encountered. The name of the dish reflects the city's name in Arabic, Dar-el-Beida (white house). See recipe, p. 51. (Fr. *couscous aux sept légumes; couscous à la viande et aux sept légumes*)

seksu belbula barley couscous. (Fr. *semoule d'orge*)

seksu bil hamus wa zbib dish of couscous topped with chickpeas, raisins and sometimes pieces of lamb or chicken. (Fr. *couscous aux raisins secs et aux pois chiches*)

seksu bil hut couscous with fish. This dish is enjoyed in the **REGIONAL CLASSIC** coastal cities along the Atlantic Ocean. (Fr. *couscous aux poissons*)

seksu bil qemrun couscous with shrimp.

seksu ger^ca hamra couscous with lamb and pumpkin.

seksu khlii couscous with spice-cured, sun-dried strips of beef. (Fr. *couscous au "khlii"*)

seksu ras mbakhar couscous with seven vegetables and lamb's head. It is one of several traditional dishes made with the lamb sacrificed for ^cId le-Kbir (Aid el Kebir). This four-day great Festival of Sacrifice, held 50 days after Ramadan, commemorates God's will that the Prophet Abraham sacrifice a lamb rather than his son Isaac. (Fr. *couscous á la tête de mouton*)

sellou rich, powdery mixture of ground almonds, sugar, toasted flour, aniseeds, sesame seeds and cinnamon. It is eaten with a spoon.

serrouda hearty purée made of chickpeas, flavored with onion and saffron, and served topped with melted butter.

sfinge yeast-raised doughnut typically eaten in the morning. It is **NATIONAL FAVORITE** a popular street food enjoyed with mint tea. Vendors deftly form the doughnuts by hand and deep-fry them in a large vat of hot oil. If the doughnuts are carried away to be eaten elsewhere, they are transported on a strip cut from a palm leaf and tied in a loop. Coarsely pounded sugar is sprinkled over the doughnuts before they are eaten. See recipe, p. 63, for an adaptation of the classic recipe—coating strawberries with the batter to make fritters.

sharbat bil luz almond-flavored milk drink.

sha^criya (cha^criya) bahara steamed vermicelli with sugar and cinnamon.

sha^criya (cha^criya) medfoun nest of steamed vermicelli with **NATIONAL FAVORITE** stewed meat hidden within it. Also simply called *medfoun*. See recipe, p. 47.

shebbakiya (chebbakiya) very sweet leavened pastry resembling **NATIONAL FAVORITE** an irregular coil of ribbons. It is made of dough flavored with orange-flower water and saffron that is deep-fried, dipped in hot honey and sprinkled with toasted sesame seeds. These pastries are the usual accompaniment to *harira,* the soup eaten at sundown each day during the month-long fast of Ramadan, although they are also enjoyed, with or without *harira,* any day of the year. *Shebbakiya* is also the name of another free-form pastry made from this dough, which is piped through a funnel or a pastry bag and formed into rosettes on the surface of the boiling oil. These rosettes are similarly dunked in hot honey and covered with toasted sesame seeds. Both versions of the pastry are also called *halwa shebbakiya (chebbakiya)* and *mahalkra.*

WONDERFUL **shlada (chlada) bil barba wa ma zher** grated beet salad flavored with orange-flower water.

shlada (chlada) bil felfel salad or condiment made with minced tomatoes, cucumbers, onions and hot red chile peppers dressed in oil and vinegar.

shlada (chlada) bil felfel wa hamd marked salad of roasted peppers and preserved lemons.

shlada (chlada) bil ful wa zitun salad with fava beans and olives.

shlada (chlada) bil matisha wa besla tomato and onion salad or condiment typically accompanying grilled meat and fish.

shlada (chlada) felfel meshwi grilled pepper salad.

shlada (chlada) khizu carrot salad.

NATIONAL FAVORITE **shlada (chlada) limun** orange salad. See recipe, p. 46. (Fr. *salade d'orange à la cannelle*)

shlada (chlada) matisha wa na^c-na^c chopped tomatoes flavored with mint.

shlada (chlada) meshwi (mechoui) salad of roasted tomatoes and green peppers marinated in vinegar and oil.

sikuk couscous with buttermilk.

tagine bid shabel stew with shad.

tagine bil bid stew with seasoned eggs.

tagine bil bid wa qemrun eggs with shrimp and cilantro.

tagine bil hut fish stew. See recipe, p. 60.

tagine bil kebda wa zitun stew of liver with olives.

tagine bil kelwa kidney stew.

tagine bil lahm (lehm) wa besbas lamb stew with fennel.

GREAT CHOICE **tagine bil luz wa bid** lamb stew with almonds and hard-boiled eggs.

tagine djaj bil btata hluwa chicken stew with sweet potatoes.

tagine djaj bil khizu chicken stew with carrots.

tagine djaj m'chermel chicken stew with olives and preserved lemons in a creamy sauce flavored with ginger, paprika, saffron, cumin and cilantro. Also simply called *djaj m'chermel*.

tagine el lahm felfel matisha lamb stew with green peppers and tomatoes.

tagine hut bil zitun stew of seasoned fish with olives.

tagine hut tungera stew of seasoned fish with sliced tomatoes, potatoes and green peppers.

tagine kabab maghdour (megdur) stew of meatballs in a tomato-based sauce with onions and garlic, and seasoned with paprika, cumin and cayenne pepper. Eggs are poached in the sauce in the cooking dish just before serving, and appear nestled between the meatballs. Also called *kefta bil matisha wa bid* and *kefta mkaouara*. See recipe, p. 48. (Fr. *boulettes de "kefta" aux oeufs*)   **NATIONAL FAVORITE**

tagine lham bil bdenshal lamb stew with eggplant.

tagine lham bil berquq lamb or beef stew with prunes and apples.

tagine lham bil ful lamb stew with fava beans.

tagine lahm bil gra^c taxrifin wa matisha mieb'sa lamb stew with zucchini, potatoes and sun-dried tomatoes.

tagine lham bil khizu lamb stew with carrots.

tagine lham bil khodra Fassi Fès-style lamb stew with seasonal vegetables. See recipe, p. 53.   **REGIONAL CLASSIC**

tagine lham bil quq lamb stew with artichokes. (Fr. *tajine de viande aux artichauts*)

tagine lham tafaya lamb stew with a sweet mixture of red onions, raisins, almonds and honey, flavored with saffron, cinnamon and rose water. An Andalusian-style lamb stew of the same name is flavored with ginger and saffron and has a topping of toasted almonds and wedges of hard-boiled eggs.   **DIVINE**

tagine makfoul bil mlokhia (mluxiya) lamb stew with okra and tomatoes.

tagine m'derbel stewed lamb spread with a purée of eggplant or pumpkin.

tagine m'hammar stuffed cornish hens in paprika sauce.

tagine m'qualli bil khizu wa krafes lamb stew with carrots and celery in a sauce flavored with ginger and saffron.

tagra fish preparation named for the unglazed pottery bowl in which it is made.

REGIONAL CLASSIC — **tangia Mrakchiya** bachelor's stew, a specialty of Marrakech. It is a one-dish meal made of well-seasoned meat and onions that is placed in a two-handled earthenware crock or amphora—also called a *tangia* (see illustration, p. 35)—and slowly cooked for hours on embers in a public oven.

tasira eel with raisins and onions.

NATIONAL FAVORITE — **tektuka (chakchouka)** cold tomato and sweet pepper salad. The dish is named after the bubbling sound of the mixture of seasoned chopped tomatoes in oil as it simmers and reduces to a purée without water.

temrika meslalla garlic beef with cracked green olives; served on the eve of the Sabbath in Sephardic homes.

teyhan stuffed spleen.

WONDERFUL — **tmer bil luz** dates filled with almond paste. The large *medjool* dates grown in the oases of Morocco are easy to stuff because of their size. See *Resources,* p. 71, for supplier of *medjool* dates in the United States.

NATIONAL FAVORITE — **trid** dish made with thin, circular sheets of somewhat oily pastry dough. Sheets of baked dough are layered in a *tagine* with sauce in between layers and stewed meat, generally chicken, on top of the stack. This dish is considered a primitive form of *bestila,* the classic squab pie. In the medina of Fès and elsewhere, one can watch women rolling dough for *trid* and baking it on a heated dome-like utensil called a *gedra dial trid* (see *Foods & Flavors Guide*).

NATIONAL FAVORITE — **wadnine el kadi** a folded and fried unstuffed pastry of the *rghaif* family (see *Foods & Flavors Guide*) named the "judge's ears." It is made by taking a small ball of dough and rolling it into a very thin square, which is then folded into thirds by bringing first one side then the other over the middle section. This process is repeated after rotating the strip 90 degrees, producing a square pastry about 4–5 inches wide and nine layers thick. Before it is fried, the pastry square is stretched on each of its four sides to produce uneven contours. It is eaten with a topping of sugar and cinnamon or with warm honey. Also called *miklee*.

NATIONAL FAVORITE — **zahlouk** cooked eggplant and tomato salad. See recipe, p. 44.

Menu Items in French

agneau aux artichauts et aux courgettes lamb stew with artichokes and zucchini. See recipe, p. 54. (*lham bil quq wa gra^c taxrifin*) **WONDERFUL**

agneau ou boeuf aux pruneaux et aux amandes lamb or beef stew with prunes and almonds. See recipe, p. 50. (*lham bil berquq wa luz*) **NATIONAL FAVORITE**

boulettes de "kefta" aux oeufs stew of meatballs in a tomato-based sauce with onions and garlic, and seasoned with paprika, cumin and cayenne pepper. Eggs are poached in the sauce in the cooking dish just before serving, and appear nestled between the meatballs. (*tagine kabab maghdour bil bid, kefta mkaouara, kefta bil matisha wa bid*) **NATIONAL FAVORITE**

"briouat" à la cervelle pastry triangles filled with brains. (*briwat (briouat) bil mohk*)

"briouat" au riz pastry triangles filled with sweetened rice. (*briwat (briouat) bil ruz*)

"briouat" aux "merquez" cigar-shaped pastries filled with small beef or lamb sausages heavily seasoned with paprika and cayenne pepper, which give the sausage a reddish color, along with black pepper and garlic. (*briwat (briouat) bil merguez*) **NATIONAL FAVORITE**

brochettes pieces of meat or giblets broiled on a skewer. See recipe, p. 55. (*kabab*)

brochettes de foie type of kebab in which pieces of fresh lamb's liver seasoned with cumin, paprika and cayenne are individually wrapped in sheep's caul, put on skewers and grilled over charcoal. This is one of the traditional lamb dishes eaten during ^{c}Id le-Kbir (Aid el Kebir), the four-day religious festival that includes the sacrifice of a lamb. (*boulfaf, bu-lfaf*) **NATIONAL FAVORITE**

brochettes de viande hachée minced lamb with spices, grilled on skewers. (*kefta kabab*)

cornes de gazelle crescent-shaped pastries called "gazelle's horns," which are filled with almond paste. Only a very thin shell of pastry encases the filling. Orange-flower water is added to the dough and often to the almond paste as well. See recipe, p. 64. (*ka^{c}b el ghzal*) **NATIONAL FAVORITE**

couscous á la tête de mouton couscous with seven vegetables and lamb's head. It is one of several traditional dishes made with the lamb sacrificed for ᶜId le-Kbir (Aid el Kebir). This four-day great Festival of Sacrifice, held 50 days after Ramadan, commemorates God's will that the Prophet Abraham sacrifice a lamb rather than his son Isaac. (*seksu ras mbakhar*)

couscous à la viande et aux sept légumes Casablanca-style couscous with seven different seasonal vegetables and meat. See *couscous aux sept légumes*. (*seksu* Beidaoui)

couscous au "khlii" couscous with spice-cured, sun-dried strips of beef. (*seksu khlii*)

REGIONAL CLASSIC **couscous aux poissons** couscous with fish. This dish is enjoyed in the coastal cities along the Atlantic Ocean. (*seksu bil hut*)

couscous aux raisins secs et aux pois chiches dish of couscous topped with chickpeas, raisins and sometimes pieces of lamb or chicken. (*seksu bil hamus wa zbib*)

NATIONAL FAVORITE **couscous aux sept légumes** Casablanca-style couscous with seven different seasonal vegetables and often meat. The vegetables are arranged in radial fashion on a mound of couscous, with the meat on the peak. It is considered good luck to have seven vegetables in the preparation, but more or less than seven also will be encountered. The name of the dish reflects the city's name in Arabic, Dar-el-Beida (white house). See recipe, p. 51. (*seksu* Beidaoui)

"khlii" au citron spice-cured, sun-dried strips of beef with lemon. See *Foods & Flavors Guide*. (*khlii bil limun*)

NATIONAL FAVORITE **"khlii" aux oeufs** spice-cured, sun-dried strips of beef with eggs. See *Foods & Flavors Guide*. (*khlii bil bid*)

GOOD CHOICE **lentilles au courges et "khlii"** lentils with pumpkin and spice-cured, sun-dried strips of beef. (ᶜ*des bil gerᶜa hamra wa khlii*)

lentilles au "khlii" lentils with spice-cured, sun-dried strips of beef. (ᶜ*des bil khlii*)

poisson en tajine "m'qualli" *tagine* of fish in a sauce flavored with ginger and saffron and garnished with preserved lemons. (*hut m'qualli*)

poisson farci au riz fish stuffed with rice. (*hut mᶜammar bil ruz*)

poulet aux oeufs *tagine* of chicken cooked in a sauce flavored with saffron, flat-leaf parsley and cinnamon. Before serving the stew, a mixture of beaten eggs seasoned with cumin is added, which, when cooked, makes the dish omelet-like. (*djaj m'kaddem, djaj souiri*)

poulet aux tomates et au miel tagine of lamb or chicken in a sauce of honey-sweetened tomatoes. (*djaj matisha m'sla*) DIVINE

poulet "k'dra" aux pois chiches et aux oignons chicken with chickpeas and onions, flavored with saffron and paprika. (*djaj k'dra bil besla*)

poulet "mᶜammar" farci au couscous chicken stuffed with couscous. (*djaj mᶜammar bil k'seksu*)

poulet "meslalla" chicken with cracked green olives. (*djaj bil zitun meslalla*)

poulet "m'qualli" tagine of chicken flavored with ginger and saffron. (*djaj m'qualli*)

poulet "m'qualli" au citron comfit tagine of chicken with olives and preserved lemons in a sauce flavored with ginger and saffron. See recipes, pp. 56–58. (*djaj m'qualli bil hamd marked wa zitun*) NATIONAL FAVORITE

salade d'orange à la cannelle orange salad flavored with cinnamon and orange-flower water. See recipe, p. 46. (*shlada limun*) NATIONAL FAVORITE

semoule d'orge barley couscous. (*seksu belbula*)

soupe de dchicha au blé soup made with crushed grains of wheat. (*chorba bil dshisha*)

soupe de gombos au "khlii" soup-like dish made with spice-cured, sun-dried strips of beef (*khlii*), beans and dried, powdered okra and flavored with paprika. (*mlokhia bil khlii*)

soupe de semoule au "nafaᶜ" semolina soup flavored with aniseed. (*nafaᶜ*)

tajine aux côtes de chardons meat stew flavored with pale-green stems of the wild thistle, which are notoriously difficult to trim of tough parts. (*gernina, garnina*) REGIONAL FAVORITE

tajine aux courgettes "slaouia" et "mlokhia" lamb with squash and okra. (*lham bil slaouia wa mlokhia*)

tajine de "kabab maghdour" stew of bone-in or boneless lamb cooked with onions, cumin and paprika. The name of the dish means "cheating" kebabs, acknowledgment of the fact that the meat has not been grilled on skewers. (*kabab maghdour*)

tajine de "kabab maghdour" aux oeufs stew of bone-in or boneless lamb cooked with onions, cumin and paprika, with eggs poached in the sauce just before serving. (*kabab maghdour bil bid*)

tajine de viande aux artichauts lamb with artichokes. (*tagine lham bil quq*)

tajine de viande aux courgettes lamb with zucchini squash, flavored with *za^ctar*, a wild herb of the thyme and oregano family. (*lham bil gra^c taxrifin wa za^ctar*)

REGIONAL CLASSIC **tajine de viande aux oignons** sweet lamb stew seasoned with ginger. It is dressed with onion rings cooked in *smen* (aged butter) and olive oil, and flavored with saffron and cinnamon. *Kamama* is a specialty of Meknès. (*kamama*)

viande de mouton à la vapeur steamed mutton. (*choua*)

Foods & Flavors Guide

This chapter is a comprehensive list of foods, spices, kitchen utensils and cooking terminology in transliterated Moroccan Arabic, with English translations. The list will be helpful in interpreting menus and for shopping in the lively and fascinating outdoor markets. As a rule, market (*souk*) vendors do not identify their wares with signs, so it would be useful to learn how to say, "What is this called?" See *Helpful Phrases*, p. 75. Write down the answer as it sounds to you, and use this *Guide* to help identify it. Remember that Moroccan Arabic is a conversational dialect and therefore many transliterated spellings are possible. You might also get a response in one of many possible Berber dialects, which are not covered here. The sundry medicinal and grooming botanicals are beyond the scope of this book.

Several words in this list contain a consonant called ^c*ein* (^c*ain*) that is not used in English. It represents a gutteral sound that is made far back in the mouth, as in "baa" of a sheep. Common ways to write this consonant in English are with a superscripted c (^c), as used here, or a reverse apostrophe ('). The ^c can be found anywhere within a word. In this list, the ^c is ignored when alphabetizing.

The regular apostrophe (') is used in this *Guide* to indicate that a vowel between consonants has been dropped. An example is *b'stila* versus *bestila*. Some writers also use the regular apostrophe to symbolize the ^c*ein* and to denote the infrequent glottal stop in Moroccan Arabic, which commonly is described as the sound made between the two vowels in the exclamation "uh oh!" This inconsistency in transliterations can be confusing. In this list, the apostrophe is ignored when alphabetizing.

In general, the definite and indefinite articles, which are prefixed to nouns and adjectives by hyphens, are not included here. They follow complex rules and are unnecessary for our purposes. For pronunciation aids, see *Helpful Phrases,* p. 75. Also see the *Bibliography,* p. 133, for references to the Moroccan Arabic grammar text and the Moroccan Arabic/English and English/Moroccan Arabic dictionaries edited by Richard S. Harrell and Harvey Sobelman.

abachi wild cardamom with black pods.

addar bass.

aid (ᶜid) feast; celebration.

Aid el Kebir four-day great Festival of Sacrifice. See ᶜId le-Kbir.

ᶜalk t-telh generic term for gum arabic. Also see *awerwar*.

argan thorny tree (*Argania sideroxylon*) native to southwestern Morocco. Its fruit is the source of a nutty-flavored, edible oil used in the southwestern region of Morocco. See *zit argan*.

arhissa (harissa) thick, spicy condiment of Tunisian origin made with dried hot red chile peppers, olive oil and garlic.

ᶜark s-us licorice.

ᶜashek spoon; also called *mᶜelka* (*mᶜelqa*).

ᶜasir fruit juice; pomegranate, orange and lemon juices are traditional. *Ma,* which also means water, is another word for juice, but it refers to both fruit and vegetable juices.

ᶜasluj artichoke stem used in cooking; another word for artichoke stem is *kharshuf* (*xershuf*).

ᶜassal honey.

atay tea.

atay akhdar green tea.

atay b'naᶜ-naᶜ mint-flavored tea, typically made with green tea. Sprigs of fresh spearmint (*Mentha viridis*) and chunks of sugar cut from a large loaf are added to the teapot while the tea is brewing. Served at the end of a meal, this beloved beverage usually is prepared by the master of the house. At several points while the tea is steeping, he pours out a small amount into a glass and tastes it. When the tea is judged ready, the teapot is raised high above glasses set on a tray, and the tea is carefully and dramatically poured. One must wait for the glasses to cool a bit before drinking. Tea drinking is not limited to the end of a meal, however; it is enjoyed throughout the day. One no longer feels obligated to drink three glasses of tea at a sitting, as social protocol once dictated.

atay nnegru black tea; also called *atay khula*.

ᶜatriya spice or condiment.

ᶜattar seller of herbs and spices.

ᶜattug young chicken.

awerwar gum arabic, the odorless, pale-yellow resin from a tree (*Acacia senegal*). It is used in confections and confectionary coatings to prevent crystallization of sugar and as a folk medicine for certain ailments. A generic term for gum arabic is *ᶜalk t-telh*. Also see *meska,* another resin with culinary uses.

azenbu young barley shoot. It also is the name of a Berber dish of seasoned porridge or couscous prepared from barley or another grain other than wheat (see *Menu Guide*).

bakkal (beqqal) small neighborhood grocery; also called *hanut*.

bakoola (bakoula) wild greens. A common one is mallow, a nutritious spinach-like plant with large leaves. It also is the name for a cooked salad made with wild greens (see recipes, pp. 42–43). Other spellings are *bekkula* and *beqqula*.

bakur type of fig that is the first of the season to ripen.

barba beet.

bared cold.

batata (btata) potato.

bayd (bid) egg.

bayd (bid) es shabel shad roe.

bayet stale; leftover. Another word for stale is *qkim*.

bdenshal eggplant; also called *branina (braniya)*.

bebbush snail; also called *glal*.

beghrir yeast-raised pancake cooked on one side only, without oil, in a round, unglazed earthenware dish. The "uncooked," upper side is full of little holes. The pancake, traditionally enjoyed for breakfast with melted butter and honey or sugar, is also eaten as a dessert.

begri beef; also called *lham (lhem) begri*.

beida (bida, byad, byed) white.

beldi indigenous, native or homegrown. It is also the name for the native Moroccan apricot, which can be distinguished from imported varieties because its seed adheres more firmly to its flesh. The general name for apricot is *meshmash*.

beqqal (bakkal) small neighborhood grocery; also called *hanut*.

beqqula (bekkula) wild greens. A common one is mallow, a nutritious spinach-like plant with large leaves. It also is the name for a cooked salad made with wild greens (see recipes, pp. 42–43). Other spellings are *bakoola* and *bakoula*.

berquq plum, prune. Green, unripe plums are pickled in water, vinegar and salt, and eaten as a snack.

berrad pot-bellied teapot used to brew mint tea.

berrada small, unglazed ceramic jug used to keep water cool; also called *qellush*.

besbas fresh fennel bulb.

besla onion; red ones are more common.

bessila leek; also called *korrat*.

bestila (b'stila, besteeya) large and elaborate festive pie served as the first course in a *diffa*, or celebration feast. It is made with many ultrathin, round sheets of pastry dough called *warka*, and typically filled with pieces of cooked squab (often with bones) a lemony egg sauce and sweetened, toasted almonds. The more traditional squab filling can be replaced with chicken. The poultry is cooked whole in a sauce that includes onion, pepper, parsley, saffron, cinnamon and sugar. When done, it is removed from the pan, cut into pieces, usually without boning, and put on top of a few layers of pastry placed on a special round, shallow-rimmed cooking pan (*tobsil dial bestila*). The pastry should extend considerably beyond the edges of the pan to provide for adequate sealing of the pie during the last steps of its assembly. To achieve this, several single pastry circles are overlapped to form a composite layer that is larger than the pan. The highly seasoned meat layer is covered with more pastry and topped with eggs that have been scrambled in the reduced sauce the meat cooked in plus some lemon juice. Additional pastry is placed over this and covered with a mixture of ground, toasted almonds, cinnamon and granulated sugar that has been pounded to a fine powder. After this step, the pastry extending beyond the pan is brought up and folded over the top the pie before the final pastry layer is added and its edges tucked way underneath to enclose the entire pie. After the *bestila* is baked, powdered sugar is sprinkled on top and a geometric design is drawn on top of that with cinnamon.

bettih (bettix) melon.

bibi turkey.

bid (bayd) egg.

bid (bayd) es shabel shad roe.

bida (beida, byad, byed) white.

bira beer.

Bismillah means "in the name of God." The word is said before each meal to ask God's blessing of the food and also to wish one a good appetite.

bit-l-makla dining room.

bled countryside.

bnin delicious.

bortuqal orange; can also be called *limun* and *letshin*.

branina (braniya) eggplant. *Branina* is also the name of a stew (*tagine*) of lamb named for the fried eggplant that garnishes it. Another name for eggplant is *bdenshal*.

brek duck.

brik savory filled pastry of Tunisian origin similar to the *briwa* (see this Guide). The filling typically contains eggs, often with cilantro and parsley, spiked with a little *harissa*, a hot red paste made from chile peppers. The pastry must be eaten immediately after it is fried, and the egg should remain runny.

briq coffee pot.

briwat (briouat) small, plump triangles made of thin sheets of pastry dough (*warka*) wrapped around sweet or savory fillings. (The singular form of *briwat* is *briwa*.) To make them, a spoonful of filling is placed near one end of a strip of lightly oiled pastry. Either corner of the pastry where the filling was placed is picked up and put over the filling. This triangle-shaped portion is then raised and folded over onto the adjacent part of the pastry sheet, maintaining the triangular shape in the process. The triangle continues to fatten as it is folded back and forth until the end of the pastry sheet has been reached. Any loose ends are tucked inside before the pastry is baked or deep-fried. *Briwat* can also be rectangular or cigar-shaped.

bsibsa (bsibissa) mace.

b'stila (besteeya, bestila) large and elaborate festive pie served as the first course in a *diffa*, or celebration feast. It is made with many ultrathin, round sheets of pastry dough called *warka*, and typically filled with pieces of cooked squab (often with bones) a lemony egg sauce and sweetened, toasted almonds. The more traditional squab filling can be replaced with chicken. After the *bestila* is baked, powdered sugar is sprinkled on top and a geometric design is drawn on top of that with cinnamon. See *bestila* for details on assembling the pie.

btata (batata) potato.

btata hluwa sweet potato.

btata qesbiya Jerusalem artichoke; also simply called *qesbiya*.

buboinott (bubanett) large (about 3-inch diameter), foot-long sausage filled with organ meat.

bu-dra old, strong-flavored or rancid *smen*, the salted butter that is sometimes clarified and aged.

bu-et-tob date with a small pit.

bu-jnuba crab.

bu-mqusa lobster.

bussera variety of sweet lemon (*Citrus limetta*) having a characteristic, nipple-like end. It is used to make preserved lemons (see *hamd marked*).

bu-ᶜwida pear; also called *lingas*.

buzrug (buzruq) mussel. It is eaten only if cooked for about an hour.

byad (beida, bida, byed) white.

chaᶜriya (shaᶜriya) vermicelli. It is steamed like couscous and served with meat, used in soup or enjoyed topped with cinnamon and sugar. Also called *fdawesh*.

chermula (shermula) highly seasoned "dry" marinade for fish or meat, which varies from region to region and is likely to contain onion, garlic, cilantro, flat-leaf parsley, saffron, paprika, hot red pepper, cumin, and a little olive oil and lemon juice. For game, the saffron may be replaced with cinnamon, or cinnamon, raisins and honey.

chiba (shiba) absinthe, a bright-green, distilled spirit of wormwood and many other herbs and spices, which is banned in most Western countries. Wormwood (*Artemisia absinthium*) is the source of a bitter, dark-green oil believed to contain psychoactive and/or toxic compounds.

chlada (shlada) salad.

chorba (shorba) light soup without thickeners such as flour, yeast or eggs. It sometimes has large-grained couscous (*mhammsa*) in it. Also called *subba*.

chtato wooden-hooped sieve with a flat bottom made of silk, which is used to sift very fine flour for pastries. A similar sieve called a *gorbal* (*ghorbal*) has a coarse wire mesh bottom and is used to sort couscous granules by size.

chuaya (shuwwaya) grill for broiling meats and fish.

dafi warm.

danun yogurt.

dar felfel Indian long pepper. The pungent berries resemble elongated peppercorns. They are ground and typically included in the spice mixture called *ras l-hanut*.

dar sini true cinnamon (Ceylon cinnamon). *Karfa* (*qarfa*) is cassia (Chinese cinnamon), a similar spice frequently confused with true cinnamon.

dellah watermelon; also called *kuwwar*.

der^ciya sea perch.

^cdes lentil.

dgig (dqiq) flour; usually means wheat flour. *Farina* and *thin* are other names for wheat flour.

diffa celebration feast of many courses for important events such as births and weddings.

dik rooster. Another name for rooster is *farooj*.

djaj chicken.

djaja hen.

doqq variety of small, thin-skinned lemon (*Citrus limonium* Risso) used in making preserved lemons (see *hamd marked*).

dra corn; also called *dra hamra*.

dra bida sorghum. It is ground and made into a soup or porridge of the same name. The dish typically is flavored with olive oil and thyme or cumin.

Sorghum is grown in the High Atlas Mountains and in the southwest. Another name for sorghum is *illane* (*iliane*).

dshisha cracked wheat or barley used to make porridge; also the name of the porridge (see *Menu Guide*).

fakya (fakiya) fresh or dried fruit.

fanid candy.

farina wheat flour; also called *dgig* (*dqiq*) and *thin*.

farooj rooster. Another name for rooster is *dik*.

fdawesh vermicelli. It is steamed like couscous and served with meat, used in soup or enjoyed topped with cinnamon and sugar. Also called *shaᶜriya* (*chaᶜriya*).

feggus (feqqus) long, slightly ridged cucumber with less water and fewer seeds than the common variety of cucumber grown in the United States.

felfel (felfla) generic term for pepper, including the spice and the fleshy varieties.

felfel abyad white pepper.

felfel akhal black pepper. Also called *ibzar* and *lebzar*.

felfel hamra sweet red pepper, paprika. Also called *felfel hluwa*.

felfel harra hot red pepper, cayenne. Also called *felfel sudaniya*.

felfel hluwa sweet red pepper, paprika. Also called *felfel hamra*.

felfel mrakad pickled sweet green peppers.

felfel sudaniya hot red pepper, cayenne. Also called *felfel harra*.

felfel xedra green pepper.

feqqus (feggus) long, slightly ridged cucumber with less water and fewer seeds than the common variety of cucumber grown in the United States.

ferran communal oven where families bring their bread to be baked. The loaves are stamped with an identifying mark. However, bakers work in the same neighborhood oven over a long time and have little difficulty identifying which loaves belong to each of their customers—mark or no mark.

fersheta fork; also called *garfu* and *mtshekka*.

fershiya bottle cork.

ferx tall, round basket with a handle; used to transport and sell mulberries (see illustration, p 26).

fess egg yolk.

festeq pistachio nut.

fjel (fjila) radish; also called *lefjel*.

fjel le-xla horseradish.

113

fliyya (fliou) wild mint (pennyroyal) consumed as an herbal tea. Although ingestion of concentrated pennyroyal oil can be toxic, normal consumption of pennyroyal tea is harmless.

fogga^c mushroom.

frach pigeon.

frik fresh, young corn. It is also the name for cracked green wheat or barley, which is fried and eaten only when the mature grains are not available.

frit fried potatoes (chips); French fries.

fti tender.

ftur breakfast.

ful fava bean.

ful gnawa black-eyed pea.

fwad viscera.

gamila small saucepan.

garfu fork; also called *fersheta* and *mtshekka*.

gazuza carbonated soft drink.

gda lunch.

geddid strip of preserved meat.

gedra (gdra) bottom part of a *couscoussier*, a two-part cooking pot made of aluminum, stainless steel or earthenware. The *gedra* or lower part is used to cook stews. The *keskas* or top part is a tight-fitting, colander-like pot with a perforated bottom in which couscous granules are cooked and flavored by steam escaping from the stew simmering in the lower pot.

gedra dial trid domed ceramic utensil used for cooking thin, circular sheets of a somewhat oily pastry dough for the dish called *trid*. This dish is considered a primitive form of *bestila*, the classic squab pie (see *bestila*, this *Guide*).

gelmi (genmi) mutton.

gemh wheat. Wheat flour is called *dgig* (*dqiq*), *farina* and *thin*.

ger^ca (gra^c, qra^c) hamra pumpkin or squash; also simply called *ger^ca* (*gra^c, qra^c*).

ger^ca (gra^c) slaoui long, pale-green, slightly curved squash; also simply called *slaoui* (*slawi, slawiya*).

gerga^c walnut; also called *guz*.

gernina (garnina) wild thistle, a relative of the globe artichoke, which is available only in early spring. The plant's pale-green stems are trimmed of leaves and tough fibers, chopped into little pieces and cooked with meat and preserved lemons in a stew (*tagine*) of the same name. The stems impart a bitter flavor and are thought to be good for the liver.

gerrab water seller, who typically is colorfully dressed and has metal drinking cups dangling on his costume. Today he appears to do a better business getting tips for photos than selling water.

gers small loaf of bread.

gezzar butcher.

glal snail; also called *bebbush*.

gorbal (ghorbal) wooden-hooped sieve with flat wire meshwork at the bottom, which is used to sort couscous granules and to separate grain from husk. A similar sieve called a *chtato* has a silk bottom and is used to sift very fine flour for making pastries.

gouza sahrawiya grains of paradise—small and pointed reddish-brown seeds with a peppery taste. They are ground and typically included in the spice mixture called *ras l-hanut*.

graᶜ(gerᶜa, qraᶜ) hamra pumpkin or squash; also simply called *graᶜ (gerᶜa, qraᶜ)*.

graᶜ (gerᶜa) slawiya long, pale-green, slightly curved squash; also simply called *slawiya (slawi, slaoui)*.

graᶜ taxrifin (tixrifin) zucchini squash.

gsaa large, round, flat dish made of earthenware or wood, which is used to make couscous granules and knead bread dough. Also called *kesria (qesriya)*.

gtar plate or dish.

guz walnut; also called *gergaᶜ*.

guza nutmeg.

habb grain.

habbet hlawa aniseed; also simply called *hlawa*.

habb le-mluk cherry.

halba (helbah) fenugreek.

halouf (helluf) pig (pork is not eaten by Muslims).

halwa (helwa) sweets (cakes, cookies or candy).

hamd lemon; also called *limun*.

hamd marked preserved lemon, one of the characteristic ingredients of Moroccan cooking. The rind is cut into pieces and added toward the end of the cooking process; the pulp is blended in with the sauce. It imparts a unique, pungent flavor to many dishes. Unpreserved lemon is not a satisfactory substitute. Lemons are easily preserved at home. See recipe, p. 68. The preferred lemon varieties are the *doqq* and *bussera*. Thin-skinned fruits are good for salads and garnishes; preserved lemons with thicker skins hold up better when simmered in a stew (*tagine*). The lemons are salted, covered with freshly squeezed lemon juice, covered and marinated for several weeks. Nontraditional ingredients added along with salt can include cinnamon, cloves, garlic, and pickling spices.

hamus (hummus) chickpea.

hanut small neighborhood grocery; also called *bakkal* (*beqqal*).

harissa (arhissa) thick, spicy condiment of Tunisian origin made with dried hot red chile peppers, olive oil and garlic.

harr spicy hot.

harsha large circles (about 15 inches in diameter) of flat, unleavened Berber bread made of course semolina flour (*smida*). *Harsha* typically is sold by street vendors early in the morning.

hbeq basil.

hebra boneless meat.

hekk bristly "choke"(or "beard") from a type of artichoke (*Cynara humilis*) or cardoon (domesticated thistle, *Cynara cardunculus*) containing rennets that curdle milk to produce cheese. Connoisseurs prefer the taste of cheese produced by the chokes of *Cynara humilis*. Before chokes are added to milk, they are pounded into a paste, or dried and pulverized. Also see *raipe*.

helbah (halba) fenugreek.

helluf (halouf) pig (pork is not eaten by Muslims).

helwa (halwa) sweets (cakes, cookies or candy).

helwa delkuk macaroon-like coconut cookie.

hergma lamb or beef hock; also the name of a dish containing lamb or beef hocks.

hlawa aniseed; also called *habbet hlawa*.

hleb milk.

hleb mhers milk with a little coffee.

hleb skhun steamed milk.

hlu (hluwa) sweet.

hmada sour.

hmam pigeon, squab (young pigeon).

hmer red.

hrur hot sauce.

hsab bill.

hshel partridge.

hshish tender.

hummus (hamus) chickpea.

hut fish.

hut musa sole.

huta buriya gray mullet.

ibzar black pepper; also called *felfel akhal* and *lebzar*.

ᶜid (aid) feast; celebration.

ᶜId le-Kbir (Aid el Kebir) four-day great Festival of Sacrifice held 50 days after Ramadan. It commemorates God's will that the prophet Abraham sacrifice a lamb rather than his son Isaac. Throughout the country, those who can afford it sacrifice an animal, typically a sheep, in honor of this event, and many special dishes containing lamb are prepared. Kebabs made from the offal of the freshly killed animal are especially prized. Other dishes traditionally made during this religious celebration include a variety of *tagine,* or stews, with lamb and vegetables or fruits, and *mechoui,* whole, spit-roasted lamb, brushed with melted butter and a spice mixture including red and black pepper, cumin and coarse salt. The meat is slow-cooked to perfection, with a crispy crust on the outside and tender, melt-in-the-mouth meat on the inside.

ᶜId s-Sgir celebration at the end of Ramadan when alms, especially wheat, are given to the less fortunate. People eat a lot of sweets during this celebration.

ikerdasen homemade Berber sausage. Several types of meat are rubbed with a mixture of coriander, white pepper, paprika, cumin, saffron and salt, and dried in the sun for a few days. The meat is then chopped into small pieces, seasoned with more of the spice, and stuffed into casings. Also called *kurbass.*

iklil firm cheese made from a type of yogurt called *raipe,* which is produced from milk thickened by the bristly "chokes" (or "beards") of wild artichokes. The mixture is set aside for three to four days before being put into a cheesecloth bag and squeezed to remove the moisture. With the addition of salt, the cheese lasts longer. A softer cheese (*jben*) results if the mixture sits for only a day before being squeezed.

illane (iliane) sorghum. It is ground and made into a soup or porridge typically flavored with olive oil and thyme or cumin. Sorghum is grown in the High Atlas Mountains and in the southwest. Sorghum and the porridge made from it are also called *dra bida.*

Imouzzer non-carbonated bottled mineral water (brand name). Other brand names of non-carbonated bottled mineral water available are Sidi Ali and Sidi Harazem. Oulmes is a brand of carbonated bottled mineral water.

ᶜineb grape.

jaban taffy or nougat.

jben cheese, typically indigenous Moroccan salted or unsalted farmer's cheese. It can be a soft, spreadable cheese of uniform consistency or firmer with small cavities. Farmer's cheese made in the Rif Mountains is salted and often sold in little shallow baskets.

jebbana large serving bowl.

jelban pea.

jelfa rind.

jenjlan (zenjlan) sesame seed. The seeds typically are toasted before use.

kabab (kebab) pieces of meat, commonly lamb, cooked on skewers.

kabar (kebbar) caper.

kabbad fragrant, oblong, thick-skinned lemon (*Citrus medica*) with small sections, which is used to flavor tea and make jams.

kamun cumin.

kanaria (qennariya) domesticated thistle, or cardoon (*Cynara cardunculus*), a relative of the globe artichoke. The stalks of the plant are trimmed of leaves, thorns, and tough fibers, cut into small pieces and cooked along with meat and preserved lemons in a stew also called *kanaria*. Another name for cardoon is *lkama*.

kanun small charcoal brazier made of unglazed earthenware, iron or copper, which typically is set on the floor. Round ones are used to cook a *tagine* and to make ultrathin leaves of dough called *warka* on a flat pan (*tobsil dial warka*) placed over the hot coals. Rectangular ones are used to grill skewered meat. A brazier is also called a *mejmar*.

karamus type of fig that ripens late in the season.

karfa (qarfa) cassia (Chinese cinnamon). True cinnamon is called *dar sini*.

karkum turmeric, used mainly as food coloring. Powdered turmeric mixed with trace amounts of powdered saffron is sold in small paper packets and routinely added to many dishes. When affordable, saffron threads also are added to the stew pot. Also called *quekum*.

kas drinking glass.

kaskrut sandwich.

kawkaw peanut.

kbal ear of corn; also called *mezgur*.

k'dra classic yellow sauce made with meat stock, aged butter (*smen*), onions, pepper, butter, saffron and additional flavorings as desired.

kebab (kabab) pieces of meat, commonly lamb, cooked on skewers.

kebbaba bitter, hot berries of the cubeb pepper plant (*Piper cubeba*), included in the Moroccan spice blend called *ras l-hanut*.

kebbar (kabar) caper.

kebda liver.

kefta ground meat.

kelwa kidney.

kermus fig.

kermus en-nsara prickly pear, or Barbary fig; also simply called *kermus*.

kerwiya caraway.

kesbur (qesbur) coriander leaves (cilantro) and seeds.

keshshina kitchen; also called *kuzina* and *metbex*.

keskas (kskas) top part of a *couscoussier*, a two-part cooking pot made of aluminum, stainless steel or earthenware. The *gedra* or lower part is used to cook stews. The *keskas* or top part is a tight-fitting, colander-like pot with a perforated bottom in which couscous granules are cooked and flavored by steam escaping from the stew simmering in the lower pot.

kesra round, leavened, flat Moroccan bread; also see *khobz. Kesra* also means the alms or "handout" (such as a piece of bread) one would give a beggar.

kesria (qesriya) large, round, flat dish made of earthenware or wood, which is used to make couscous granules and knead bread dough. Also called *gsaa*.

kettara metal apparatus used to distill orange-flower water or rose water.

khabia (xabya) earthenware butter churn.

khal (khula) black.

kharshuf (xershuf) artichoke stem used in cooking; also called ᶜ*asluj.*

khdenjal greater galangal, a fleshy rhizome or root-like stem that looks like ginger root and has a hot, peppery taste. The dried root is ground and typically included in the spice mixture called *ras l-hanut.*

khder (khodra, xder, xedra, xodra) the color green; also can refer to a vegetable or to undercooked meat.

khess (xess) lettuce.

khizu (xizzu) carrot.

khlii spice-cured, sun-dried strips of beef stored in fat until needed. To prepare *khlii,* strips of meat about an inch square are rubbed with a mixture of salt, garlic and ground cumin and coriander seeds, marinated overnight in this spice blend and then dried in the sun. Once dried, the strips are cooked in beef fat mixed with some olive oil and water, and boiled until the water completely evaporates. They are removed from the oil and cooled, put into jars and covered with liquified fat. After the fat solidifies, the jars are tightly closed. Meat preserved by this method keeps for over a year. The preserved meat is cooked in a stew (*tagine*) with vegetables, eggs or couscous.

khobz traditional round, leavened, flat loaf of crusty Moroccan bread, which is about eight to ten inches wide, one to two inches thick, and very absorbent. Cut wedges or torn pieces of bread are used with the fingers of the right hand as utensils to pick up food. Since most homes do not have an oven, bread is baked in a large communal oven. Unbaked loaves prepared at home are given an identification mark, placed on a wooden board and covered with a cloth. Children typically carry the loaves to the oven. Also called *kesra*.

khodra (khder, xder, xedra, xodra) the color green; also can refer to a vegetable or to undercooked meat.

khukh (xux) peach.

khula (khal) black.

khyar cucumber.

kina quinine.

knelba syrup made with orange-flower water.

kordas tripe.

korrat leek; also called *bessila*.

kouclas dumpling made of rice or bread.

krafes celery.

kromb cabbage or cauliflower; another word for cauliflower is *shiflur*.

kronfel (qronfel) clove; also called *ud el nuar*.

k'seksu couscous; see *seksu*.

kskas see *keskas*.

kurbass homemade Berber sausage. Several types of meat are rubbed with a mixture of coriander, white pepper, paprika, cumin, saffron and salt, and dried in the sun for a few days. The meat is then chopped into small pieces, seasoned with more of the spice, and stuffed into casings. Also called *ikerdasen*.

kuskus couscous. It is the Arabic word for the dry grain product—small granules made of semolina—as well as the preparation of granules steamed and often covered with a stew (*tagine*), with the whole arranged into a pyramid. The Berber name for couscous is *seksu*, and the Moroccan Arabic term is *k'seksu*. Couscous is Morocco's national dish, and as such there are countless variations of it, including sweet ones served for dessert (see *seksu*, this *Guide*).

kuwwar watermelon; also called *dellah*.

kuzina kitchen; also called *keshshina* and *metbex*.

labyad egg white.

laglas ice cream.

lamuri cod.

laᶜuq marmalade; jam.

lben buttermilk. It typically is made by letting fresh milk curdle naturally. When the curdled milk is churned, butter separates out of the mixture. The liquid remaining is buttermilk. The milk can also be curdled by adding the hairy "choke" (or "beard") of or dried wild artichokes.

ldid delicious.

lebzar black pepper; also called *felfel akhal* and *ibzar*.

lefjel radish; also called *fjel (fjila)*.

left turnip.

lehmenn green crabapple.

letshin orange; can also be called *limun* and *bortuqal*.

lham (lhem) meat; lamb. Butchered animals in markets typically are males, still bearing testicles to prove that the meat is not from females. Moroccans claim the ability to distinguish a taste difference between the meat of male and female animals of comparable age. They avoid eating meat from female animals, believing it both unsavory and unhealthy. If anyone wants to purchase just the testicles, the butcher will not sell them because the (sexual) origin of the remaining meat will no longer be certain. Another reason meat from females is scarce in markets is that females are not butchered until their fecundity and milk production ebbs.

lham (lhem) begri beef; also called simply *begri*.

lham (lhem) d-le-ᶜjel veal.

lham (lhem) jmel camel meat.

lham (lhem) l-helluf pork (not eaten by Muslims).

lham (lhem) maᶜzi goat meat; also called simply *maᶜzi*.

lim lime.

limun small green Moroccan lemon; *limun* also can refer to an orange. Also called *hamd*.

lingas pear; also called *bu-ᶜwida*.

lkalᶜ napkin.

lkama domesticated thistle, or cardoon (*Cynara cardunculus*), a relative of the globe artichoke. The stalks of the plant are trimmed of leaves, thorns, and tough fibers, cut into small pieces and cooked with meat and preserved lemons. Another name for cardoon is *kanaria (qennariya)*.

lkelia popcorn.

louisa lemon verbena. This herb is used in tea or infusions to give a bitter-sweet taste, and is thought to improve blood circulation.

lubya (lubia, loubia) beida haricot, or kidney bean.

lubya (lubia, loubia) xodra string bean.

luz almond.

luz mfenned candied almond.

lwani dish; kitchen utensil.

ma water or juice; also see *ᶜasir.*

ma bared cold water.

maᶜdnus parsley.

mahar clam.

ma harr undrinkable water.

mahya colorless aniseed-flavored fig brandy brewed by the Sephardic Jews in Morocco. It is available commercially.

makla food; also means meal.

ma ma'dani mineral water.

mᶜammar stuffed.

maᶜquda omelet.

marak *tagine* (stew) of vegetables.

ma skhun hot water.

mᶜassala (mᶜsla) with honey. It often refers to a condiment of tomato jam that is sweetened with honey. See *matisha mᶜsla, Menu Guide,* and recipe, p. 45.

mataybsh bezzef rare (undercooked).

matisha tomato.

matisha mieb'sa sun-dried tomato.

maᶜun dish, pot or pan.

ma ward rose water distilled from petals of rosebuds. It is used to flavor pastries and is also sprinkled on the hands after a meal. There is a large center for production of rose water in the Dadès Valley. *Ma ward* is also called *ma de-l-ward.*

ma zher orange-flower water distilled from flowers of bitter oranges. It is used to flavor a variety of dishes. Also simply called *zher.*

maᶜzi goat meat; also called *lham (lhem) maᶜzi.*

m'chermel classic red sauce made by combining the following three sauces in varying proportions: *k'dra, m'qualli* and *m'hammer* (see this *Guide*).

mdaker testicle.

mehraz brass mortar and pestle used to grind herbs and spices.

mejhul variety of date.

mejmar charcoal brazier. Round ones are used to cook a *tagine* and to make ultrathin leaves of dough called *warka* on a flat pan (*tobsil dial warka*) placed over the hot coals. Rectangular ones are used to grill skewered meat. A brazier is also called a *kanun.*

melha salt.

melj leg of lamb.

mᶜelqa (mᶜelka) spoon; also called *ᶜashek.*

meqla frying pan.

meqla dial trab round and slightly concave, unglazed earthenware dish or griddle used over a charcoal brazier. A pancake called *beghrir* and flat breakfast pastries, such as *rghaif,* are fried without oil in a *meqla dial trab.*

meqli (mqliya) fried.

meqrej long-spouted kettle used for heating water.

merdeddush marjoram.

merguez Tunisian-style small, reddish beef or lamb sausages heavily seasoned with paprika, cayenne pepper, black pepper and garlic.

merina long, mottled, brown and yellow eel-like fish.

merla whiting.

merqa gravy or sauce made with cooked meat juices.

merr bitter.

meshmash apricot. The native Moroccan apricot is also called *beldi.*

meshrub soft drink; also called *munada.*

meshwa grill for broiling.

meshwi roasted.

meska (mska) mastic, an aromatic resin (hardened sap) from a tree (*Pistacia* sp.) native to the Mediterranean basin. It is powdered and added to stews and other savory dishes. Almond pastes and certain sweet dishes also are flavored with mastic. Also see *awerwar,* another resin with culinary uses.

meski muscat grape.

mesluq (mesluqa, msluq) hard-boiled (egg).

metbex kitchen; also called *keshshina* and *kuzina.*

mezgur ear of corn; also called *kbal.*

mgerfa (mgorfa) wooden spoon or ladle, typically carved from a piece of orange or lemon wood. The classic soup served at the end of each day to break the fast during Ramadan—*harira* (see *Menu Guide*)—is eaten with a *mgerfa* of lemon wood. It has a characteristic round, deep bowl and a straight cylindrical handle with a tapered end (see illustration, p. 10).

m'ghazel skewer for grilling meat; also called *qetban (qotban, quodban)* and *seffud.*

m'hammer classic red sauce containing paprika, cumin and butter.

mhammsa large (3 mm or greater) hand-rolled couscous granules made from wheat. They require longer steaming to become light and tender.

miduna round, shallow woven basket used in making couscous granules; also called *tbak.*

mlokhia (mluxiya) okra. It often is cooked with little quinces. Okra is also dried and powdered for use as a thickener.

mohk (muhkt) brain; also the name of a salad with brains.

moz banana.

mqliya (meqli) fried.

m'qualli classic yellow sauce containing saffron, ginger and olive oil and/or peanut oil.

mrina moray eel.

mska (meska) mastic, an aromatic resin (hardened sap) from a tree (*Pistacia* sp.) native to the Mediterranean basin. It is powdered and added to stews and other savory dishes. Almond pastes and certain sweet dishes also are flavored with mastic. Also see *awerwar,* another resin with culinary uses.

msluq (mesluq, mesluqa) hard-boiled (egg).

mssus sour; unseasoned.

mterrba scrambled.

mtshekka fork; also called *fersheta* and *garfu.*

muhkt (mohk) brain; also the name of a salad with brains.

mul mussel.

munada soft drink; also called *meshrub.*

mus knife.

nabka honey date.

nafaᶜ fennel seed.

naᶜ-naᶜ mint. Spearmint (*Mentha viridis*) is the most common variety. Fresh stalks of mint are considered a necessary flavoring in brewing tea.

ness-ness drink of half coffee, half milk.

noxxal bran.

nuiura (noioura, nouiouira) allspice.

nun eel.

Oulmes carbonated bottled mineral water (brand name). Brands of non-carbonated bottled mineral water are Imouzzer, Sidi Ali and Sidi Harazem.

qaᶜqulla cardamom.

qarfa (karfa) cassia (Chinese cinnamon). True cinnamon is called *dar sini.*

qehwa coffee.

qehwa bil hleb coffee with milk.

qehwa khula black coffee.

qehwa mhersa coffee with a little bit of milk.

qelb heart.

qellush small, unglazed ceramic jug used to keep water cool; also called *berrada*.

qemrun shrimp.

qennariya (kanaria) domesticated thistle, or cardoon (*Cynara cardunculus*), a relative of the globe artichoke. The stalks of the plant are trimmed of leaves, thorns, and tough fibers, cut into small pieces and cooked along with meat and preserved lemons in a stew also called *qennariya*. Another name for cardoon is *lkama*.

qesbiya Jerusalem artichoke, also called *btata qesbiya*.

qesbur (kesbur) coriander leaves (cilantro) and seeds.

qeshra peel, rind or pod.

qesriya (kesria) large, round, flat dish made of earthenware or wood, which is used to make couscous granules and knead bread dough. Also called *gsaa*.

qetban (qotban, quodban) spit; skewer. Can also mean meat on skewers. Also called *m'ghazel* and *seffud*.

qim type of small quince. Also see *sferjel*.

qkim stale; also called *bayet*.

qniya rabbit.

qorb sea carp.

qostal chestnut.

qotniya dried food such as beans and peas.

qraᶜ gourd; also means bottle.

qraᶜ (gerᶜa, graᶜ) hamra pumpkin or squash; also simply called *qraᶜ* (*gerᶜa, graᶜ*).

qronfel (kronfel) clove; also called *ud el nuar*.

quekum turmeric; see *karkum*.

quodban (qetban, qotban) spit; skewer. Can also mean meat on skewers. Also called *m'ghazel* and *seffud*.

quq globe artichoke.

raipe type of yogurt made from milk thickened by the bristly "chokes" (or "beards") of certain artichokes or thistles. If the mixture sits for a day and then is put into a cheesecloth bag and squeezed to remove the moisture, a soft farmer's cheese (*jben*) is obtained. If the mixture rests for three to four days before being squeezed, a harder cheese called *iklil* is made. Addition of salt extends the shelf life of the cheese. Also see *hekk*.

ras l-hanut literally means "head of the shop" and is a spice shop's choice blend of a myriad ground spices and herbs. It may contain components thought to be aphrodisiacs, such as Spanish fly, the crushed, dried body of the emerald-green blister beetle (*Cantharis vesicatoria* or *Lytta vesicatoria*). Most mixtures will probably include cumin, fenugreek, mace, nutmeg, cloves, allspice, cinnamon, ginger, cardamom, berries of the cubeb pepper plant (*kebbaba*), black pepper, Indian long pepper (*dar felfel*), turmeric, greater galangal (*khdenjal*), cayenne, coriander seed, grains of paradise (*gouza sahrawiya*), rosebuds and lavender. The spice mixture is used to flavor several dishes, including *mrouzia* (see *Menu Guide*) and dishes featuring game.

rashasha metal dispenser (usually ornate) with a rounded bottom and long, straight spout, which is used to sprinkle fragrant orange-flower or rose water on one's hands after a meal.

rghaif generic name for a group of flat breakfast pastries made with yeast-raised dough that is rolled thin, folded into various shapes and fried. Oil or melted butter, and sometimes sweet or savory fillings, are spread on the surface of the dough before folds are made. A favorite filling is *khlii,* sun-dried, spice-cured strips of beef. Dough can also be drawn out into threads and wound into bundles that are pressed flat and fried. See *melowi* (*milwi*), *mtsimen*, *roztel kadi* and *wadnine el kadi (miklee), Menu Guide*.

rijla purslane. The leaves are used to make *bakoola,* a dish of cooked greens. Uncooked leaves appear in some salads.

romman pomegranate.

rutal octopus, squid.

ruz rice.

sahur (shur) pre-dawn meal eaten before the day's fast begins during Ramadan.

salma sage.

seffa fine; also the name for delicate couscous granules about 1 mm in diameter made by hand-rolling coarse semolina flour (*smida*) moistened with water. While larger particles of couscous (*seksu* and *mhammsa*) are made using both *smida* and very fine semolina flour, the flour component is omitted in making the smaller couscous granules. *Seffa* is used primarily for sweet dishes, often served with buttermilk or yogurt.

seffud skewer for grilling meat; also called *m'ghazel* and *qetban (qotban, quodban).*

sekkum asparagus.

seksu couscous. It is the Berber term referring to both the dry grain product—small granules made of semolina—as well as a preparation of granules steamed and often covered with a *tagine,* or stew, with the whole arranged into a pyramid. The Arabic name for couscous is *kuskus,* and the

Moroccan Arabic term is *k'seksu.* Couscous is Morocco's national dish, and as such there are countless variations of it, including sweet ones served for dessert. It traditionally is served on Friday, the Islamic Sabbath, as a one-course family meal following the early afternoon prayers. For a *diffa,* or celebration feast, it is the last of many courses preceding dessert.

To make couscous granules, both coarse and very fine particles (flour) of semolina plus a little salt are moistened with water. The mixture is rubbed with a circular motion of the fingers against the bottom of a round, flat dish (*gsaa*) and then, using the same procedure, in a round, woven basket (*tbak*). See color insert. In skilled hands, the mixture coalesces into small particles of fairly uniform size without the use of wooden-hooped sieves to ensure uniform granules of the desired dimension, usually about 2 mm in diameter. Once formed, the granules are steamed twice, uncovered, in the top part (*keskas*) of a *couscoussier.* After steamings, the couscous granules are spread out in a flat pan until cool and worked with the fingers to remove any lumps. The granules are then air dried and stored until use. Also hand-rolled are bigger granules (*mhammsa*), 3 mm in diameter or larger, which require longer steaming to become tender, and finer ones (*seffa*), about 1 mm in diameter, that are used for delicate dishes. Couscous most frequently is made of semolina from durum wheat, but preparations are also made using other grains such as barley, corn and millet.

Families traditionally serve couscous in a large communal dish. It is eaten with the fingers, which looks easy, but isn't. A small amount of couscous and bits of the other ingredients in the preparation are picked up with the thumb and first two fingers of the right hand, and transferred to the palm of the hand. With gentle movement of the cupped hand, the food is tossed up and down, which quickly produces a neat little ball that is popped into the mouth with the same fingers used to take it from the bowl.

selq chard.

serdin (serdil) sardine.

sferjel quince. Also see *qim*.

ᶜsha supper; evening meal.

shabel shad. This popular fish is becoming a rarity because its habitat (river estuaries) has been jeopardized by overfishing and by increased levels of salinity due to upriver dams.

shahiya appetite.

sharbat popular fruit or nut-milk drink of Egyptian origin served to celebrate joyful events.

shaᶜriya (chaᶜriya) vermicelli. It is steamed like couscous and served with meat, used in soup or enjoyed topped with cinnamon and sugar. Also called *fdawesh*.

shawniya red pepper.

sheh herb with tiny, bitter, pale gray-green leaves that grows in the High Atlas Mountains. It is said to be good for the heart and liver.

sheklat chocolate.

shermula (chermula) highly seasoned "dry" marinade for fish or meat, which varies from region to region and is likely to contain onion, garlic, cilantro, flat-leaf parsley, saffron, paprika, hot red pepper, cumin, and a little olive oil and lemon juice. For game, the saffron may be replaced with cinnamon, or cinnamon, raisins and honey.

shiba (chiba) absinthe, a bright-green, distilled spirit of wormwood and many other herbs and spices, which is banned in most Western countries. Wormwood (*Artemisia absinthium*) is the source of a bitter, dark-green oil believed to contain psychoactive and/or toxic compounds.

shiflur cauliflower; also called *kromb*.

sh^cir barley.

shiyy broiled meat.

shlada (chlada) salad.

shorba (chorba) light soup without thickeners such as flour, yeast or eggs. It sometimes has large-grained couscous (*mhammsa*) in it. Also called *subba*.

shrab wine.

shtun anchovy.

shur (sahur) pre-dawn meal eaten before the day's fast begins during Ramadan.

shuwwaya (chuaya) grill for broiling meats and fish.

shwa steamed meat.

Sidi Ali non-carbonated bottled mineral water (brand name). Other brands of non-carbonated bottled mineral water are Imouzzer and Sidi Harazem. Oulmes is a brand of carbonated bottled mineral water.

Sidi Harazem see Sidi Ali.

siniya three-legged metal tray for the utensils and ingredients needed to prepare mint tea (*atay b'na^c-na^c*).

skhun hot.

skinjbir ginger. The spice is used dried and can be purchased as a powder or as dried roots.

slaoui (slawi, slawiya) long, pale-green, slightly curved squash; also called *ger^ca (gra^c) slaoui*.

smen salted butter that is sometimes clarified before being aged, often with dried herbs, in earthenware pots. Old, strong-flavored or rancid *smen* is called *bu-dra*. Visitors to Morocco find the strong, cheesy flavor of aged butter an acquired taste.

smida coarse semolina particles used to make the small-granule couscous called *seffa*.

sokkar sugar.

sokkar de-l-qaleb loaf sugar.

sokkar mqaret cube sugar.

sokkar sanida granulated or powdered sugar.

souk (suq) market, usually outdoors. Some are held on a specific day of the week and travel from place to place; others are held daily in the same location.

subba light soup without thickeners such as flour, yeast or eggs. It sometimes has large-grained couscous (*mhammsa*) in it. Also called *chorba* (*shorba*).

susis sausage.

tafaya honey-sweetened sauce with lots of red onions sautéed until limp and then cooked with honey, raisins, almonds, saffron and sometimes a little rose water. This caramelized topping is served on meat dishes. Sometimes quartered hard-boiled eggs are added for decoration.

tagine slaoui (slawi, slawiya) two-piece, glazed earthenware cooking dish consisting of a flat, shallow-rimmed round bottom and a conical cover. It is used to cook and serve Moroccan stews of the same name. Both are also simply called *tagine* (see illustration, p. 7).

t^cam food.

tamarrat "beard of an old man," an aromatic, gray-green lichen sold in outdoor markets in the south (*souss*). Today it primarily is used in perfumery, but can be a flavorant for tea, stews and couscous dishes in southern Morocco.

taouas large Chinese-style porcelain dish.

tas metal bowl with handles, used to catch water poured over the hands for washing before and after a meal.

tassargal bluefish.

tawa saucepan.

tayeb ripe.

tayeb mezyan (meat cooked) well done.

tbak round, shallow woven basket used in rolling and separating couscous granules; also called *miduna*.

tbiqa (tbicka, tbeq) large, colorful round woven basket with a conical lid, used to store and serve bread.

tebsil (tobsil) plate.

tebsil (tobsil) dial warka flat, shallow-rimmed circular pan used bottom-side up over hot embers to make ultrathin, almost transparent sheets of pastry called *warka*. In the top-side-up position, the pan can be used to bake dishes made with *warka,* such as the classic squab pie called *bestila* (see this *Guide*). A similar pan called *tebsil (tobsil) dial bestila,* which has a shallower rim, is also used to bake this pie.

tedouira thickening agent used to give body to *harira,* the classic soup served at the end of each day to break the fast during Ramadan. *Tedouira* usually consists of a mixture of flour or yeast and water, which sometimes is allowed to ferment slightly before use.

tedwira tip (for waitstaff).

teffah apple.

telj ice.

temr date.

tenjra metal cooking pot.

ᶜter herb.

terfas white Moroccan truffle, an especially prized mushroom used in Sephardic cuisine.

terrada flat grill for making the thin, circular sheets of somewhat oily pastry dough used to make the classic preparation *trid* (see *Menu Guide*).

terrah young boy employed to carry loaves of bread from homes to the public ovens and back.

tertuga ashtray.

therfist unleavened Berber flatbread made in sheets.

thin wheat flour; also called *dgig* (*dqiq*) and *farina.*

tifur large serving tray.

tikida carob; also called *xerrub.*

tin dried fig.

tizbibint black olive with a large pit.

tka taᶜ soup stock.

tobsil (tebsil) plate.

tobsil (tebsil) dial warka flat, shallow-rimmed circular pan used bottom-side-up over hot embers to make ultrathin, almost transparent sheets of pastry called *warka.* In the top-side-up position, the pan can be used to bake dishes made with *warka,* such as the classic squab pie called *bestila* (see this *Guide*). A similar pan called *tobsil* (*tebsil*) *dial bestila,* which has a shallower rim, is also used to bake this pie.

trawa fresh.

tum garlic.

tun tuna.

tunnert leavened Berber bread made in a round earthen oven that is open on the top and on one side. A flat, circular slab of dough is pressed to the inside wall and baked, yielding a curved loaf.

tut beldi mulberry.

tut rumi strawberry.

ud el nuar clove; also called *kronfel* (*qronfel*).

warka (werqa) ultrathin, almost transparent sheet of pastry made of small, overlapping circles of dough. A sheet is made by taking a ball of dough about the size of a tennis ball and tapping it repeatedly on a heated round metal pan (*tobsil dial warka*) until the entire surface of the pan is covered. Each tap leaves a small circle of paper-thin dough on the pan, and by having each small circle slightly overlap the adjacent one, a sheet the size of the pan is produced. The dough cooks quickly and is carefully lifted off the surface of the pan. Several sheets are used to make the classic squab pie called *bestila* (see this *Guide*) and many other savory or sweet dishes.

warkia leaf. It is also the generic name given a wild plant with fleshy green leaves that are cut up and cooked in the soup or porridge called *felalia* (see *Menu Guide*).

warqat mussa bay leaf.

werqa (warka) ultrathin, almost transparent sheet of pastry made of small, overlapping circles of dough. See *warka*.

xabya (khabia) earthenware butter churn.

xder (xedra, xodra, khder, khodra) the color green; also can refer to a vegetable or to undercooked meat.

xeddar vegetable seller.

xerrub carob; also called *tikida*.

xershuf (kharshuf) artichoke stem used in cooking; also called *ᶜasluj*.

xess (khess) lettuce.

xizzu (khizu) carrot.

xmira leavening agent; yeast.

xortal oats; oatmeal.

xux (khukh) peach.

yedd t-tas kettle used to pour water over the hands to cleanse them before a meal. The water is collected in a basin called a *tas*.

zaᶜfran saffron; also called *zaᶜfran el horr,* or genuine saffron. Crocus plants that are the source of this costly spice are grown in the countryside surrounding the southwestern village of Taliouine and harvested in late fall. Most of the spice is exported to Europe. The village has a saffron co-operative with a small exhibit (in French) and packets of saffron for sale. Moroccans love the flavor and yellow color that saffron imparts to food, but many cannot afford it. They use a substitute marketed under the name "colorant alimentaire synthetique," which is a brilliant orange powder containing ground turmeric and other ingredients, including a hint of saffron.

za^ctar (za^cter) wild herb of the thyme and oregano family found in the High Atlas Mountains. It is used to flavor *smen* (salted butter that is clarified and aged) and certain dishes.

zbib raisin.

zebda sweet butter made from fresh milk that has been curdled and churned. It is enjoyed fresh or used to make *smen,* salted butter that is sometimes clarified and aged.

zenjlan (jenjlan) sesame seed. The seeds typically are toasted before use.

zher orange-flower water; see *ma zher.*

zit oil.

zit argan oil from fruits of the thorny, drought-resistant argan tree (*Argania sideroxylon*) native to southwestern Morocco. The olive-sized fruits have a thin layer of flesh covering a hard nut bearing up to three oil-rich seeds. The high-quality, edible oil extracted from the seeds smells like walnuts and is a much-prized substitute for olive oil in this part of Morocco. The oil, typically produced in small amounts by families, can be purchased in southwestern markets. It is used in making pastries, for dipping bread and with almonds to make an almond butter called *amlou* (see recipe, p. 67). The fruits also provide food for goats, which climb up the trees to nibble the flesh off the nut. Travelers are amused to see trees along the roadside filled with feeding goats. Clever goat herders keep their flocks close to the highways and augment their income with tips from tourists taking advantage of the photo opportunity (see illustration, p. 38).

zit l-^cud olive oil.

zitun olive.

zitun meslalla preserved cracked green olives.

Bibliography

Adamson, Melitta Weiss, editor. *Food in the Middle Ages: A Book of Essays*. New York: Garland Publishing, Inc., 1995.

Ahmed, M. Salah, Gisho Honda and Wataru Miki. *Herb Drugs and Herbalists in the Middle East*. Tokyo: Institute for the Study of Languages and Cultures of Asia and Africa, 1979.

Barbour, Nevill. *Morocco*. London: Thames and Hudson Ltd., 1965.

Bellakhdar, Jamal. *La Pharmacopée Marocaine Traditionnelle: Médecine Arabe Ancienne et Savoirs Populaires*. Paris: Ibis Press, 1997.

Bellakhdar, Jamal, Gisho Honda and Wataru Miki. *Herb Drugs and Herbalists in the Maghrib*. Tokyo: Institute for the Study of Languages and Cultures of Asia and Africa, 1982.

Benayoun, Aline. *Casablanca Cuisine: French North American Cooking*. London: Serif, 1998.

Bennani-Smires, Latifa. *La cuisine marocaine . . . plus*. Casablanca: Société d'Edition et de Diffusion AL MADARISS, 1991.

Bidwell, Margaret and Robin Bidwell. *Morocco: The Traveller's Companion*. London: I. B. Tauris & Co., Ltd., 1992.

Bober, Phyllis Pray. *Art, Culture, and Cuisine: Ancient and Medieval Gastronomy*. Chicago: The University of Chicago Press, 1999.

Bovill, E. W. *The Golden Trade of the Moors*. London: Oxford University Press, 1968.

Bowles, Paul. *Morocco*. New York: Harry N. Abrams, Inc., 1993.

Brett, Michael and Elizabeth Fentress. *The Berbers*. Oxford: Blackwell, 1966.

Buitelaar, Marjo. *Fasting and Feasting in Morocco: Women's Participation in Ramadan*. Oxford: Berg Publishers, 1993.

Burke, James. *Connections*. London: Macmillan London Ltd., 1978.

Burke, James. *The Day the Universe Changed*. Boston: Little, Brown and Company, 1985.

Canby, Courtlandt with Arcadia Kocybala. *A Guide to the Archaeological Sites of Israel, Egypt and North Africa*. New York: Facts on File, 1990.

Canetti, Elias. *The Voices of Marrakesh: A Record of a Visit.* New York: The Seabury Press, 1978.

Carrier, Robert. *A Taste of Morocco: A Culinary Journey with Recipes.* New York: Clarkson N. Potter, Inc., 1987.

Clark, Bryan. *Berber Village: The Story of the Oxford University Expedition to the High Atlas Mountains of Morocco.* London: Longmans, Green and Co Ltd., 1959.

Collins, Roger. *Early Medieval Spain: Unity in Diversity, 400–1000,* 2nd edition. New York: St. Martin's Press, 1995.

Cowan, George D. and R. L. N. Johnston. *Moorish Lotos Leaves: Glimpses of Southern Marocco.* London: Tinsley Brothers, 1883.

Day, Irene F. *The Moroccan Cookbook.* Greta, Louisiana: Pelican Publishing Company, Inc., 2000.

Facciola, Stephen. *Cornucopia: A Source Book of Edible Plants.* Vista, California: Kampong Publications, 1990.

Field, Michael and Frances Field. *A Quintet of Cuisines.* New York: Time-Life Books, 1970.

Gellner, Ernest and Charles Micaud. *Arabs and Berbers: From Tribe to Nation in North Africa.* London: Gerald Duckworth and Co., Ltd., 1973.

Gibb, H.A.R., editor and translator. *Travels of Ibn Battuta,* A.D. 1325-1354, vol. I. (Translated with revisions and notes from the Arabic text edited by C. Defrémery and B.R. Sanguinetti.) Cambridge: Cambridge University Press, 1958.

Gibb, H.A.R., editor and translator. *Travels of Ibn Battuta,* A.D. 1325-1354, vol. II. (Translated with revisions and notes from the Arabic text edited by C. Defrémery and B.R. Sanguinetti.) Cambridge: Cambridge University Press, 1962.

Gibb, H.A.R., editor and translator. *Travels of Ibn Battuta,* A.D. 1325-1354, vol. III. (Translated with revisions and notes from the Arabic text edited by C. Defrémery and B.R. Sanguinetti.) Cambridge: Cambridge University Press, 1971.

Gibb, H.A.R., editor and translator. *Travels of Ibn Battuta,* A.D. 1325-1354, vol. IV. (Translated with revisions and notes from the Arabic text edited by C. Defrémery and B.R. Sanguinetti.) London: The Hakluyt Society, 1994.

Gitlitz, David M. and Linda Kay Davidson. *A Drizzle of Honey: The Lives and Recipes of Spain's Secret Jews.* New York: St. Martin's Press, 1999.

Guinaudeau, Z. Translated from the French by J. E. Harris. *Traditional Moroccan Cooking: Recipes from Fez.* London: Serif, 1994.

Harrell, Richard S. *A Short Reference Grammar of Moroccan Arabic.* Washington D.C.: Georgetown University Press, 1962.

Harrell, Richard S., editor. *A Dictionary of Moroccan Arabic: Arabic–English.* Washington, D. C.: Georgetown University Press, 1966.

Harris, Jessica B. *The Africa Cookbook: Tastes of a Continent.* New York: Simon & Schuster, 1998.

Hart, David M. *Tribe and Society in Rural Morocco*. London: Frank Cass Publishers, 2000.

Helou, Anissa. *café morocco*. Lincolnwood, Illinois: Contemporary Books, 1999.

Jenkins, Nancy Harmon. *The Mediterranean Diet: A Delicious Alternative for Lifelong Health*. New York: Bantam Books, 1994.

Landau, Rom. *Invitation to Morocco*. London: Faber and Faber Ltd., 1953.

Laroui, Abdallah. *The History of the Maghrib: An Interpretive Essay*. Princeton, New Jersey: Princeton University Press, 1977.

Marks, Copeland. *The Great Book of Couscous: Classic Cuisines of Morocco, Algeria and Tunisia*. New York: Donald I. Fine, Inc., 1994.

Marks, Copeland. *Sephardic Cooking: 600 Recipes Created in Exotic Sephardic Kitchens from Morocco to India*. New York: Donald I. Fine, Inc., 1992.

Maxwell, Gavin. *Lords of the Atlas: The Rise and Fall of the House of Glaoua 1893–1956*. New York: E. P. Dutton & Co., Inc., 1966.

Mayne, Peter. *The Alleys of Marrakesh*. Boston: Little, Brown and Company, 1953.

Meakin, Budget. *The Land of the Moors: A Comprehensive Description*. London: Swan Sonnenschein & Co., Lim., 1901.

Meakin, Budget. *The Moorish Empire: A Historical Epitome*. London: Swan Sonnenschein & Co., Lim., 1899.

Meakin, Budget. *The Moors: A Comprehensive Description*. London: Swan Sonnenschein & Co., Lim., 1902.

Mernissi, Fatima. *Dreams of Trespass: Tales of a Harem Girlhood*. Reading, Massachusetts: Perseus Books, 1994.

Miki, Wataru. *Index of the Arab Herbalist's Materials*. Tokyo: Institute for the Study of Languages and Cultures of Asia and Africa, 1976.

Morse, Kitty. *Come with Me to the Kasbah: A Cook's Tour of Morocco*. Casablanca: Editions SERAR, 1989.

Morse, Kitty. *Cooking at the Kasbah: Recipes from My Moroccan Kitchen*. San Francisco: Chronicle Books, 1998.

Morse, Kitty. *North Africa: The Vegetarian Table*. San Francisco: Chronicle Books, 1996.

Munson, Henry, Jr. *The House of Si Abd Allah: The Oral History of a Moroccan Family*. New Haven, Connecticut: Yale University Press, 1984.

Nelson, Harold D., editor. *Morocco: A Country Study,* 5th edition. Washington, D.C.: U. S. Government Printing Office, 1985.

Noakes, Greg and Laidia Chouat Noakes. Couscous: The Measure of the Maghrib. In *Aramco World,* Volume 49, Number 6 (November/December), edited by Robert Arndt, pp. 16–23. Houston: Aramco Services Co., 1998.

Porch, Douglas. *The Conquest of Morocco*. New York: Alfred A. Knopf, 1983.

Raven, Susan. *Rome in Africa*. London: Evans Brothers Limited, 1969.

Roden, Claudia. *The Book of Jewish Food: An Odyssey from Samarkand to New York*. New York: Alfred A. Knopf, 1999.

Roden, Claudia. *The New Book of Middle Eastern Food*. New York: Alfred A. Knopf, 2000.

Rogerson, Barnaby. *A Traveller's History of North Africa*, 2nd edition. New York: Interlink Books, 2001.

Shatzmiller, Maya. *The Berbers and the Islamic State: The Marinid Experience in Pre-Protectorate Morocco*. Princeton, New Jersey: Markus Wiener Publishers, 2000.

Shaw, Thurstan, Paul Sinclair, Bassey Andah and Alex Okpoko, editors. *The Archaeology of Africa: Food, Metals and Towns*. London: Routledge, 1995.

Seward, Pat. *Cultures of the World: Morocco*. New York: Marshall Cavendish Corporation, 1995.

Slavin, Kenneth and Julie Slavin. *The Tuareg*. London: Gentry Books Ltd., 1973.

Sobelman, Harvey and Richard S. Harrell, editors. *A Dictionary of Moroccan Arabic: English–Arabic*. Washington, D. C.: Georgetown University Press, 1963.

Sonnenfeld, Albert, editor. *Food: A Culinary History from Antiquity to the Present*. New York: Columbia University Press, 1996.

Spencer, William. *Historical Dictionary of Morrocco*. Metuchen, New Jersey: The Scarecrow Press, Inc., 1980.

Spencer, William. *Morocco: The Land and the People*. Philadelphia: J. B. Lippincott Company, 1973.

Sternberg, Rabbi Robert. *The Sephardic Kitchen: The Healthful Food and Rich Culture of the Mediterranean Jews*. New York: HarperCollins Publishers, 1996.

Tannahill, Reay. *Food in History*. New York: Stein and Day, 1973.

Tolliver, Catherine. *Moroccan Horizons*. Casablanca: Les Impressions EDITA, 1952.

Vaidon, Lawdom. *Tangier: A Different Way*. Metuchen, New Jersey: The Scarecrow Press, Inc., 1977.

van Gelder, Geert Jan. *God's Banquet: Food in Classical Arabic Literature*. New York: Columbia University Press, 2000.

Walden, Hilaire: *the moroccan collection: traditional flavors from northern africa*. San Francisco: SOMA Books, 1998.

Wharton, Edith. *In Morocco*. Hopewell, New Jersey: The Ecco Press, 1996.

Wolfert, Paula. *Couscous and Other Good Food from Morocco*. New York: Harper & Row, Publishers, 1973.

Wolfert, Paula. *Mediterranean Cooking*, rev. edition. Harper Perennial, 1994.

Woodward, Sarah. *Moorish Food: Mouth-Watering Recipes from Morocco to the Mediterranean*. London: Kyle Cathie Limited, 1998.

Wright, Clifford A. *A Mediterranean Feast. The Story of the Birth of the Celebrated Cuisines of the Mediterranean, from the Merchants of Venice to the Barbary Corsairs, with More Than 500 Recipes*. New York: William Morrow and Company, Inc., 1999.

Index

INDEX

ORDER FORM

Use this form to order additional copies of **Eat Smart in Morocco** or to order any of the other fine guidebooks in the **EAT SMART** series.

Please send me:

_____ copies of **Eat Smart in Brazil:** How to Decipher the Menu, Know the Market Foods & Embark on a Tasting Adventure

_____ copies of **Eat Smart in Indonesia:** How to Decipher the Menu, Know the Market Foods & Embark on a Tasting Adventure

_____ copies of **Eat Smart in Mexico:** How to Decipher the Menu, Know the Market Foods & Embark on a Tasting Adventure

_____ copies of **Eat Smart in Morocco:** How to Decipher the Menu, Know the Market Foods & Embark on a Tasting Adventure

_____ copies of **Eat Smart in Poland:** How to Decipher the Menu, Know the Market Foods & Embark on a Tasting Adventure

_____ copies of **Eat Smart in Turkey:** How to Decipher the Menu, Know the Market Foods & Embark on a Tasting Adventure

Each book is $12.95. Add $2.50 postage for one book, $1.00 for each additional book. Wisconsin residents add 5% sales tax. For international orders, please inquire about postal charges.

Check enclosed for $ _____

Please charge my: VISA_____   MASTERCARD_____

Card # _____ Exp. Date: _____

_____
Signature

Name: _____

Address: _____

City: _____ State: _____ Zip: _____

Telephone: _____

Email: _____

Mail this form to: **Ginkgo Press™ Inc.**
2018 Chamberlain Ave.
Madison, Wisconsin 53705
Tel: 888-280-7060 Fax: 608-233-0053
http://www.ginkgopress.com
info@ginkgopress.com

design   Ekeby
cover design   Susan P. Chwae
color separations   Widen Enterprises
printing   Thomson-Shore, Inc.

typefaces   Garamond Simoncini and Helvetica Black
paper   60 lb Joy White